FROM
SKY GIRL
TO
FLIGHT
ATTENDANT

THIRD WORLD RESOURCES
The Data Center
464 19th Street
Oakland, CA 94612 USA

FROM
SKY GIRL
TO
FLIGHT
ATTENDANT

Women and the Making of a Union

GEORGIA PANTER NIELSEN
Introduction by Alice H. Cook

ILR Press
New York State School of Industrial and Labor Relations
Cornell University

Cover design: Kathleen Dalton, Brownhouse Design

Cover photograph: courtesy of Association of Flight Attendants

Library of Congress number: 82-8210
ISBN: 0-87546-093-3 (cloth)
        0-87546-094-1 (paper)

Cataloging in Publication Data

Nielsen, Georgia Panter, 1937–
    From sky girl to flight attendant.

    Includes index.
    1. Association of Flight Attendants (U.S.)
I. Title.
HD6079.2.U5N53   1982   331.88'11387742'0973
ISBN 0-87546-093-3   82-8210
ISBN 0-87546-094-1 (pbk.)

Copies may be ordered from
ILR Press
New York State School of
Industrial and Labor Relations
Cornell University, Box 1000
Ithaca, NY 14853

To my mother-in-law, Magda, and
her son Dan, my husband

Contents

Acknowledgments

This book owes much to my mother-in-law, Magda Nielsen. Magda, without the benefits of the revival of feminism that occurred in the late 1960s, was able to impress upon her children the value of discarding many traditional views of male and female roles. Rearing her son Dan, who became my husband, Magda ensured that he knew how to cook and to perform household tasks in addition to his intellectual and sports pursuits. Largely due to Dan's support and encouragement, I have had the time to research and to write this work.

The ideas for the book were the result of San Jose State University incorporating women's studies into its curriculum. I was able to enroll in this program during the mid-1970s as a re-entry student. A short report for a history class of women in twentieth-century America led to a thesis for a master of arts degree at that university. This book is an outgrowth of that thesis.

Many people gave assistance, scholarly and personal. The faculty at the history department at San Jose State University including professors Charles Burdick, Billie Jensen, David Eakins, Edgar Anderson, David McNeil, Barbara Dubins, and Frances Keller gave encouragement and assistance as I wrote on women's topics. Professor Charles Kunsman of the political science department also gave me assistance.

Edith Lauterbach, a flight attendant with United Airlines and early union officer, was the first to offer her experiences through an interview. Remaining available throughout the course of my research, she provided documents and helped trace other sources. My thanks also go to Ada J. Brown Greenfield, founder and first president of the Air Line Stewardesses Association, for her personal account of the origins of the union. Diane Robertson, a longtime union worker and flight attendant with United Airlines, supplied many glimpses of the development of the union. Additionally, Kathy Hutchens, a local union officer, provided an ongoing account of historical precedents as they were being applied in the real world.

I also thank the national officers and staff of the Association of Flight Attendants in Washington, D.C., for their cooperative effort in the cause of my work from 1976 to the completion of the book. Rowland K. Quinn, Jr., executive secretary of the National Mediation Board, gave interviews and was available for verification of facts.

The industrial relations department of United Airlines at Elk Grove Township, Illinois, supplied data, and Chuck Thomson, director of industrial relations, gave interviews and helped to reconstruct recent history of flight attendants on United Airlines. He also directed me to individuals who would serve as memory banks.

Attempts to research flight attendant history have taken me from coast to coast and to the Hawaiian Islands, prying into people's recollections of social, labor, and union history. Documents and photographs have appeared with surprising regularity. I am indebted to the many United Airlines flight attendants for their generous cooperation in sharing their own personal accounts. Their insights have supplemented my own experiences as a flight attendant for United Airlines since 1960 and as a union member since about the same time.

My work would not have evolved into this book but for the attention given to it by four people at Cornell University. Jean McKelvey, professor emerita, and Charles Rehmus, dean of the New York State School of Industrial and Labor Relations, critiqued my work. Frances Benson and Holly Bailey of the Publications Division of the school guided the manuscript through many stages of promotion, editing, and production.

My special thanks go to Alice Cook, professor emerita, Cornell University, for the introduction to this book. She put the story into national and international perspective on the status of women within the labor movement.

Many union representatives quickly learn that history does not repeat itself and that facts never speak for themselves. Most historians share those views, and it is within that context that I assume the full responsibility for the contents of this book.

Introduction

The story told here is unique in at least two respects. It is an account of the recent feminization of an occupation, which draws attention to the problems special to women working in it; and it is the history of women organizing and maintaining a union with a predominantly female constituency.

Over the last few years, the number of women members of unions has been growing steadily and in many unions far exceeds the number of men enrolling. Moreover, a substantial part of labor force growth has been among women working in trades and occupations that until now were only minimally organized—government employees and service and white-collar workers of all kinds—and these women are now forming unions or unionlike organizations both inside and outside the official labor movement.

Although unions are the self-advertised agents of change, they have been among the last of the power centers in industrial society to recognize what Ralph Smith calls the "subtle revolution" of women's mass entrance into the labor force over the last fifteen years (*The Subtle Revolution*, Washington, D.C.: Urban Institute, 1980). Their entry into unions has been equally large and unsettling. While women still remain proportionately less well organized than men, their numbers in the unions have grown more rapidly than men's. In the United States, as well as in a number of other industrialized countries, their addition to union rolls has saved the unions, in some cases, from an absolute loss of members and, generally, from disastrous losses at a time when the labor force was expanding.

Thus, the issue of women's place in the labor movement is a pressing one, which is in process of definition and only slowly and uncertainly approaching solution. Shall women organize their own unions? Are they ready yet to assume leadership in the tough world of labor relations, where they must negotiate contracts, handle grievances, and defend their organizations against rival unions and employer antiunionism? When and how can they become competent to undertake these tasks? Is the appropriate answer integration into a male-dominated organization, symbolizing as it must the solidarity of the sexes in a common struggle and causing reliance on the trained experts and the sometimes vast accumulated resources of the established unions? Do the men want this? Are they ready to accept the implications of equal treatment of women and the addition of women's issues to an already crowded and imperative agenda?

The numbers and proportions of women in unions would have increased more rapidly but for a number of characteristics of American unions. Chief among these is that American unions have not traditionally been very successful in organizing workers in white-collar and service jobs, where women have mainly found employment. Yet it is these expanding trades that have been responsible for the labor market pull on women, a pull at least as powerful as any push from women themselves to enter the labor force.

The unions' general lack of response to their growing female membership is also attributable to their history as predominantly male institutions. In the United States unions had their origins in the crafts—among printers, construction workers, miners, railroad workers, seafarers, teamsters, bakers, grain millers, machinists, firefighters, post office employees—and these crafts were all male. In the late nineteenth century when unions were getting established, women's work was limited to an even narrower range of occupations than it is today. They were janitresses, laundresses, bindery workers, waitresses, and shop clerks, but mainly they were domestic servants. Some were beginning to be clothing workers, shoe workers, glove makers, and textile operatives. Even in those trades where men also worked, they were isolated in women's occupations. They worked as finishers and sewing machine operators but not cutters or pressers, weavers and inspectors but not spinners.

To the extent that women were eligible and acceptable in unions, the unions were, with very few exceptions, led entirely by men who accepted women as second-class workers, earning a special women's wage. To be sure, from time to time they adopted resolutions about equal pay for equal work but only rarely implemented them.

In many cases, women were barred from union membership by a constitutional provision that the organization was open to "white males of good moral character"; the constitution of the Air Line Pilots Association contained such a clause as late as 1942. Like the pilots' organization, some unions found a place for the women in special membership classifications or special sections or branches, auxiliary bodies without power to influence, much less control, the union's policies and development. Some union-minded women set up their own all-female unions and, in the United States as well as Britain, the Women's Trade Union League to bring together all the isolated groups of women within the labor movement. Few of the all-women's unions survived very long, and none of them in this country lasted into this century (in Ireland and Denmark such unions still exist almost as historic artifacts). Some amalgamated with men's unions and became subsidiary bodies. A few kept their identity in trade locals (buttonhole makers or women teachers) within the national or regional union body, or even functioned as nationwide locals, as did the stewardesses who joined the Transport Workers Union. But for the most part, women simply became individual members within larger male-dominated organizations.

Why did the men take the women at all? They were not in the same trades, and they were thus hardly rivals for scarce jobs. Within the working class, they were another caste. It was quite acceptable to pay them wages lower than the lowest-paid man received, a common practice in union as well as nonunion shops. Unions, like employers, accepted these "women's wages" as appropriate for unskilled hands and for persons not committed to the labor force—women, it was well known, would work for only a few years before marriage or to earn pin money after it. Women's very admittance to unions and their status within them rested on these assumptions.

But there was a rub. Women's deftness, their dexterity, indeed their docility recommended them to employers. Gradually they entered trades formerly closed to them. Employers broke down trades into occupations, jobs, and tasks, for which minimal training sufficed. Occupations that were formerly men's undisputed turf became feminized. It took only a few years at various periods of industrial history for cigar and garment making, office work, and inflight service each to become women's work. Once women took over, the occupation became, of course, low paid and offered little or no career or promotional possibility. The unions' function became strongly that of drawing and defending demarcation lines, so as to protect as long as possible the conditions and status of the skilled male worker. The inclusion of women members was an effort to control the dangerous competition their exclusion generated. Reluctantly unions accepted the finer and finer division of labor, so long as some skilled trades remained male dominions—the butcher in the supermarket, the cutter in the garment shop, and the accountant and salesman in the office.

Women's labor history has only just begun to be written, and almost everything about the way the unions dealt with what they designated the "woman question" remains to be examined. Some women's names nevertheless appear in conventional labor history. Among them are Mother Jones, Elizabeth Gurley Flynn, Rose Schneiderman, Bessie Hillman, Agnes Nestor, Rose Pisotta, Elizabeth Christman, Fannia Cohn, and Florence Hanson. Many came to prominence because the Women's Trade Union League offered them space and place for their talents. Several are known because they were members of "rival" movements threatening the increasingly conservative AFL. Most of them came out of the women's trades, that narrow band of occupations first feminized and worst exploited.

Flight attendants offer as good an example as can be found of women's entry into newly opened occupations and of the pull the airlines exerted upon young women to seek employment in this work. When commercial flying opened new occupations, the airways were already a man's territory. Men who had flown in World War I became the pilots of civilian air traffic. Women were no more expected to work in the cockpit than in the locomotive cab.

In the early days, men also dealt with passengers' needs in the cabin, and the first stewardesses, employed in the 1930s, came into what had been initially designated men's jobs. Whether the occupation was to be men's or women's work under the unwritten laws of job segregation was not finally clear, however, until World War II greatly increased commercial flying and at the same time drained men out of the labor market and into the military. Soon it was accepted that women could serve hungry passengers, soothe the airsick, and reassure the uneasy and perhaps do these things more "naturally" and successfully than men.

From the beginning the flight attendants were treated like daughters of Victorian, middle-class families, girls who needed protection during the few months they would work. It was expected, of course, that they would not question the decisions of their employers or of the captains in the cockpits, and that they would just as unquestioningly stop work after they married. The $125 a month that the United attendants earned when they first came to work in the 1930s remained the base wage there for more than fifteen years.

Only good-looking, slender, unmarried, nonpregnant women could be employed or remain employed on the airlines. The image was precisely that of the girl next door—neat, nice, and good enough for your son to marry. These standards were enforced by appearance "counselors" at the domicile cities, who weighed and sometimes measured stewardesses and checked to be sure they wore girdles, skirts, and high heels. When United added native Hawaiian men on its run to the islands, it became apparent that the weight, age, and marriage regulations did not extend to men.

The airlines' standards for women were so widely accepted in the mid-1960s that the courts handling cases under the antidiscrimination provisions of Title VII approached the marriage issue gingerly. Initially, the judiciary held that the ban on employing married women discriminated not between men and women but between married and single women and hence was not covered by the law. Arbitrators were likewise undecided. By 1968, however, courts had determined that marital restrictions indeed violated Title VII.

Even after the decisions against the no-marriage rule and United Airlines had reluctantly agreed to abandon the rule, the airline still refused to reinstate eligibles unless they dropped claims to back pay. After years of negotiation and litigation, many of these cases remain unsettled.

What personnel directors, airlines managers, and union leaders often failed to recognize was that women who work, whether married or unmarried, face a long list of problems that affect men only little if at all. The men who dominate the bargaining process and grievance handling are apt then to attach little importance to these matters, or, in all good will, do not recognize their significance to the woman union member. In the case of the flight attendants, these issues were not only the marriage and pregnancy bans and the appearance regulations, but the custom of housing two women in the same hotel room when flights kept them away overnight from their domiciles; the separate seniority lists for men and women on the Hawaii run; and the effects on women's menstrual cycles of the introduction of the jets.

One consequence of the rules on marriage and pregnancy was rapid turnover among the members of the flight attendants' union. The male pilots functioned in a realm where their skills and the severity of their admissions tests gave them a scarcity value that allowed them to make a principle of free choice of union membership; the women by contrast knew that waiting lists of hundreds of young women were available to fill vacancies caused by the no-marriage and early retirement policies. For them union security became a central condition of continuing to maintain their union. Thus, very different sets of priorities came to govern the men's and women's agendas for bargaining.

As for bargaining itself, a company that had instituted and maintained discriminatory regulations based on sex could not be expected to take a women's negotiating team quite seriously. The first women to meet the company as bargainers in 1945 were a sturdy lot. They had to wait out company delays; overcome the withdrawal of their parent union, the Air Line Pilots Association, which was unwilling to go all the way with them on some of their issues; and endure the condescension implied in the company's handling of dumb females who would wear down fast. After months of steadfast bargaining, they achieved their major goals, a limitation on flight hours and their first raise in pay since 1930.

Thirty years later in a notably similar reprise of that first bargaining session, negotiations again dragged out, this time for eighteen months, as the women's union with women negotiators struggled to achieve a tolerable recognition of their union and its demands. These two episodes should dispel the belief widely held among women as well as men that women lack the hardihood to succeed in negotiating face-to-face with major companies and in representing large, diverse constituencies.

Today, the Association of Flight Attendants (AFA) is not only one of the few unions in the world chaired and led by women, it is the only one with a predominantly female executive board and collective barginging committees. While not quite all of its members are women—indeed its 85 percent female constituency is somewhat less than that of several other unions—the women in AFA and a few small independent flight attendants' unions have emerged as leaders. This is in great contrast to the other organizations where women hold chiefly token positions on the boards and are almost invisible on the important bargining committees.

AFA has broken new ground. Other women's unions here and elsewhere were usually formed out of the necessities of isolation. Barred from the men's organizations or existing in all-female trades, women had no choice, if they were to organize, but to go it alone. AFA and its predecessor organizations have a long history of dependency upon an exclusively male union, from which they achieved independence only recently. This book details the symbiotic relationship of the pilot and the flight attendant unions, filled as it has been with tensions, dominance, anxiety, interdependence, guardianship, rivalry, and mutual distrust that existed simultaneously with mutual aid.

Surely it is not accidental that such a colorful history is in large part a product of the fact that ALPA is an exclusively male union and AFA a predominantly female organization. The two unions present a new version of the age-old war of the sexes, this time on union turf. Because the pilots were exclusively male and their occupation defined as professional, the best accommodation they could offer to women nonprofessionals was a segregated section of the union. This section repeatedly sought to gain its independence, either in the form of an autonomous unit under the aegis of ALPA or under its own charter granted by the AFL-CIO. All approaches to the AFL-CIO for an independent charter proved repeatedly disappointing. For ten years the division's male president directed much energy to these ends only to meet the predictable end of removal from office by the parent organization. Recognizing that their organization was too frail to stand alone, his loyal followers moved to the Transport Workers Union (TWU). TWU also gave them a section of their own, a national "local" of stewardesses. But their promised autonomy lasted only a few years before it was violated by the parent union.

ALPA and TWU wanted the stewards and stewardesses but feared the consequences of their affiliation. Their reasons for the inclusion of the flight attendants and their fears of it varied with the turns of events and had little to do with maintaining a strong organization of flight attendants. Rather, they seem mainly to have been concerned with preventing the group from going to a rival union or from dealing with the airlines on any but a restricted range of issues.

The problems, quarrels, and reconciliations of these unions did not, of course, exist in isolation. Rather they originated in the days of American Federation of Labor (AF of L) dominance of the labor movement and were exacerbated by the rivalry that developed between the old A F of L and the newborn Congress of Industrial Organizations (CIO) in the 1930s and 1940s.

Once A F of L and CIO merged in 1955, a proposed solution to the problems of the airborne unions, namely an amicable divorce of the flight attendants from the pilots, was prevented by the fact that the federation already had two unions with departments that housed flight attendants—the pilots were affiliated with the A F of L and the Transport Workers Union with the CIO. The federation pressed to maintain the status quo as a less troublesome alternative to chartering a new union of flight attendants that would then find itself in conflict with the jurisdictions already granted and recognized. The result of this decision and of all the counseling and guidance that George Meany, the federation president, gave ALPA about its troublesome women over a period of almost twenty years, was that, in the name of unity, the flight attendants were divided among a number of unions, some of them independent company-wide unions. Their disunity, to be sure, had causes similar in breadth and contentiousness to those pervading the whole labor movement, but also it arose out of dissatisfactions and disagreements members had with the contracts the union was able to achieve and with the administration of these less than perfect documents.

Would the parent unions' reactions have been different had the membership been predominantly male rather than female? Would it have been the same had the women adopted a stereotypical obedience and passive acceptance of male dominance? Were not both companies and national unions unused to dealing and unwilling to deal with a women's union as an equal with equal claims to varying agendas, varying priorities, and its own aggressive leaders? The accounts of the months-long bargaining sessions speak to the companies' eventual acceptance of the women with whom they dealt. The agreement finally worked out with the pilots for an independent union of flight attendants speaks for the somewhat later acceptance by at least one of the two major parent organizations.

The pivots around which union independence turned were two, as Nielsen sees them. One was the birth and growth of the movement for women's equality that touched responsive nerves in large numbers of women, employed, at home, and in school during the 1960s and 1970s. The flight attendants, already exposed daily to discrimination in treatment and in wages, were sensitive to the issues the women's movement raised and rallied to. The movement indeed reached into the trade unions fairly broadly, as the organization of the Coalition of Labor Union Women (CLUW) demonstrates. The flight attendants were early affiliates of CLUW. But many of them were members also of other women's groups outside the labor movement that were encouraging women to recognize and deal with the inequities embedded in society, the same inequities adopted and exploited by companies and unions—the "Fly Me!" advertising campaign; the compulsory retirement upon marriage; the image of an occupation as young, attractive, nurturing; the all-male, cigar-smoking executive flights served by flying "bunnies." It is indisputable that the long struggle to lift the marriage ban, deal with pregnancy as any other disability, develop a career line for

flight attendants, limit hours, and raise pay would not have succeeded
had not the whole normative set of attitudes about women and work
changed radically with the adoption of Title VII and the rise of the
women's movement.

A second turning point for the AFA was the opportunity the union's
bargaining teams sought and found in the AFL-CIO Labor Studies
Center. There the flight attendants bonded their specific experience
with a broader, generalized knowledge of collective bargaining. Their
continuing use of the center testifies to labor education's effectiveness in
building and maintaining well-led unions.

This story of a single union and its women members is in fact a
chronicle of women's changing place in the world of work and of things
to come in the labor movement.

Alice H. Cook
March 1982

From Sky Girl
to Flight Attendant

1
A History of the Stewardess's Occupation

Since the first eight women took to the skies as stewardesses in 1930, the women and few men who fly the nation's airliners as flight attendants have captured the imagination of the American public. As early as 1933, they were described by a female reporter for the Toledo, Ohio, *Sunday Times* as having been "eulogized, glorified, publicized, and fictionalized."[1]

Capitalizing on the public's interest, the airline industry has sold the flight attendant as part of its product. Discriminatory hiring policies of the airlines attempted to keep accurate a public image of youthful and beautiful people winging their way to exotic places, and the stewardess image became a highly profitable marketing commodity. While the degree and kind of exploitation varied with the times and within the industry, no U.S. carrier has escaped that particular marketing mentality. By the 1960s, the lifestyle of the stewardess was depicted in X-rated films and semipornographic literature.

As recently as 1978, an interviewer of potential flight attendants stated that a good complexion was an important qualification for being hired.[2] Most flight attendants, however, take a less superficial view of themselves. Fifty years after the initiation of their profession, they number around 50,000 nationwide and 125,000 worldwide, and they comprise approximately 15 percent of the total airline workforce in this country.[3] Sometimes called stewards, stewardesses, hostesses, or cabin attendants, they spend their work lives providing safety and comfort to the traveling public throughout the airways of the world. Their unique workplace exists in airplanes that range in speed, seating, and size from small puddle jumpers with fewer than fifty seats to wide-bodied jumbo jets capable of carrying about five hundred people up to six thousand miles nonstop at six hundred miles per hour. A few flight attendants are now working aboard supersonic airplanes with cruising speeds exceeding the speed of sound.

The inflight duties involve serving hundreds of food and beverage combinations, ranging from full-course meals in first-class sections to no-frills coach beverage services. Not only do the airlines consider meal services essential for passengers, they take for granted that most travelers enjoy dining on airplanes. Perhaps one of the greatest changes in the cabin attendant's job has been the tasks accompanying the steady increase in liquor services. Fifty years ago when the first women became flight attendants, prohibition was still in force, and by 1931 there were stern warnings that "drinking aboard planes is not permitted."[4] The airlines are now among the largest liquor vendors in the United States.

While all flight attendants spend the majority of their working hours dispensing food and beverages, the safety function of the job is given great weight in the occupation. The flight attendant is universally recognized as the primary cabin safety factor and is trained to deal with inflight or ground emergencies, including such recent phenomena as bomb threats, hijackings, and flight attendant abuse.[5]

Around forty-five thousand of the nation's flight attendants are a unionized group of working women and men who bargain collectively for almost every condition of their work lives and for many aspects of their personal lives. Among the trunk carriers serving the long-haul routes, only the flight attendants working for Delta Airlines, who number around thirty-five hundred, do not have representation through a union. To put these figures in perspective, in 1979 total employment in the U.S. airline industry was 340,696. A substantial number of these workers are unionized; among United Airlines' 49,720 employees as of February 28, 1981, approximately 60 percent were represented by labor organizations.[6]

The labor relations experience of the flight attendants is highly unusual for a historically short-term force of predominantly female workers. The origins of the vocation, the process of unionization, the 1965 enactment of Title VII of the Civil Rights Act of 1964, and the revival of feminism during the late 1960s, which affected the stewardesses as much, if not more, than any other group of working women, provide significant insight into woman's place in twentieth-century America.

The experiences of the stewardesses of United Airlines, the nation's biggest air carrier, exemplify the labor relations history of flight attendants. It was the women themselves, disenchanted with salaries and working conditions almost from the origins of the occupation, who organized. Although there had been earlier attempts, Ada J. Brown, a stewardess employed by United Airlines, first successfully organized a union for flight attendants; it received recognition in 1946. It was William A. (Pat) Patterson who, as a young assistant to the president of Boeing Air Transport (BAT), gave the go-ahead to the stewardess job in 1930. Sixteen years later, as the president of United Airlines, he signed the first union agreement between cabin attendants and an employer, thus initiating the longest labor relations history with that specific class and craft in the United States.

Commencing as an independent union, the United group allied with Western Airlines' stewardesses and continued as a fledgling unaffiliated union for four years. With the exception of several small airlines, organizations of flight attendants began as affiliated unions, mainly through the Air Line Pilots Association (ALPA); the one significant exception was the group of attendants from Pan American World Airways, which joined the Transport Workers Union (TWU) in 1946.

By the 1970s flight attendants from Continental Airlines, Pan American World Airways, American Airlines, and Trans World Airlines had broken away from their unions. Each group created an unaffiliated, independent union not unlike the Air Line Stewardesses Association founded by the United stewardesses in 1945. Perhaps predictably, the United group, having already experienced the pitfalls of independence, stayed with an affiliated union, now called the Association of Flight

3

Attendants, and represents 22,115 flight attendants on eighteen U.S. carriers.[7]

The unstable and dynamic airline industry of the 1980s is the outgrowth of several equally unstable periods. In most countries airlines began when enterprising people bought airplanes, flew them or hired pilots to fly them, and advertised for joyriders. In the United States airlines grew out of flying the mail; thus, commercial aviation began as a public enterprise initiated by the federal government. It was the Post Office Department that recognized the potential of airplanes for delivering mail, and by 1912 had begun requesting funds to experiment with delivering letters by air.

The government made appropriations to the Post Office Department by 1917 for expansion of air mail, and the postmaster general was in charge of the department's ambitious plans to deliver mail by air to most major cities. Hiring seventy-five daredevil pilots, most of them ex–military pilots with World War I experience, the postmaster general swore them in as U.S. Post Office agents. Armed with guns, and flying flimsy open-cockpit airplanes, these unusually adventurous men pioneered air commerce in the United States.

By the early 1920s some few entrepreneurs, among them young Juan Trippe, who would found and lead Pan American World Airways, sought private contracts to carry the mail. It has been suggested that by 1925 Trippe had helped persuade Representative Clyde Kelly, chairman of the House Post Office Committee, to introduce legislation to permit private operators to obtain mail contracts.[8] Eventually known as the Kelly Act, the bill passed easily, and the Post Office Department posted bids for private contractors to supplement air postal service by carrying mail on the feeder routes.

The first contracts were generally small and awarded to men interested in seat-of-the-pants flying, while the more monied Wall Street backers shied away from the still somewhat risky business. There were exceptions, such as Juan Trippe and a few well-heeled friends and former Yale classmates, who bid on and were awarded Air Mail Route No. 1, the run from New York to Boston. The new airline executives began experimenting with airplanes large enough to carry the mail, and in the political climate of the 1920s, when the president could declare,

"The business of America is business," it was only a matter of planning to bring the new commercial airline industry into a more attractive risk structure for investors. This change came quickly through the Air Commerce Act of 1926 and through congressional amendments in 1926 and 1927 to the Kelly Act.

These amendments, as well as the Air Commerce Act, were the brainchild of Dwight Morrow, "the biggest of big businessmen" and a senior partner of the Wall Street banking house of J. P. Morgan.[9] Before the new aviation legislation, Morrow had become President Coolidge's handpicked man to establish an aviation policy for America. As chairman for a newly created presidential board, Morrow submitted ideas to study aviation, to permit the government to establish and maintain airways, to expand and maintain goverment aid to contract airmail carriers, and to set up federal licensing standards for pilots and planes. Congress followed Morrow's suggestions and these measures, as well as a new method of compensating airmail carriers that doubled the indirect subsidy, were adopted. The risk level was then more acceptable to Wall Street investors.

The present-day giant airline corporation structures began taking shape. Consolidation within the new industry was rapid and well planned. The newly created commercial airline industry was given the boost it needed when Charles Lindbergh soloed across the Atlantic. Americans' fascination with aviation became a national obsession, and Lindbergh became one of the most admired heroes of the century.

Small airlines, unable to obtain financing, were failing and were usually grabbed up by the few well-financed entrepreneur industrialists who could afford to wait to acquire the plum routes. By 1930 an estimated 90 percent of all air transport operations in the United States were carried out by only four corporate groups. It had been no accident. Perhaps never had an important sector of American economic life been more directly shaped by an appointed official of government.

President Hoover's postmaster general, Walter Folger Brown, a Hamiltonian believer in strong central power, wanted to create several large transcontinental airlines within the United States. He stepped in and directed the development of the new and potentially major industry. A Republican, he envisioned a system of strongly financed, competitive, transcontinental airlines intersected by an extensive network of feeder routes. It followed that such a system would stimulate manufacturers to build the safe, fast planes that the country required for public convenience and national defense.[10]

With more than minimal influence from Postmaster Brown, the Watres Act was approved on April 29, 1930. Under the act the postmaster general might extend or consolidate routes "when in his judgment the public interest will be promoted thereby." Further, the airlines were now to be paid according to the amount of space available for mail, not according to the old pound-per-mile rate. It was an outright subsidy and a method of payment that was to have far-reaching effects. Now that the airlines were paid for space there was every advantage in ordering larger airplanes; thus the aircraft manufacturers could benefit. Brown also saw that if the airlines were ever to be able to stand on their own, they would have to install more passenger seats and attract a profitable passenger traffic business.

The enactment of the Watres Act dealt the small operators already carrying airmail the death blow. Brown later argued, "There was no sense in taking this government's money and dishing it out . . . to every little fellow that was flying around the map. . . ."[11] Response from wealthy businessmen came quickly, and a number of small operating companies involved in air transportation comprised a shopping list for Wall Street holding companies. The thirty-eight airlines that existed during 1930 and 1931 were reduced to sixteen by the end of the decade; this decrease was mostly due to mergers rather than bankruptcies. It took little imagination to predict the outcome of plans laid by financiers in partnership with the federal government, but many businessmen of limited vision did not understand that the corporate pattern for the airline industry had already been set.

One of the most notable failures of the time was Walter T. Varney. Varney had applied for and had been granted the first postal department contract in 1926. His mail route served Pasco-Boise-Elko, which is frequently described as "from nowhere to nowhere." No one else had applied for the route, but by 1933 Varney's attorney was able to negotiate a cash sale of Varney Airlines to United Air Lines for two million dollars. Varney immediately speculated in other passenger airlines, including Varney Speed Lines and a Rocky Mountain airline. Soon finding himself broke, he became a truck driver over the same rugged mountains where he had started the first airline in the United States. Primarily providing scheduled trips to deliver airmail, the companies still considered passenger comfort a by-product. (One airline, Transcontinental Air Transport (TAT), whose routes made use of segments of train travel, had been formed solely for passenger travel by the railroad companies, but by 1930 it had merged with Western Air Express due to near bankruptcy.)[12] Making multiple stops across the land, these early flying machines were unpressurized, noisy, cold, and often bumpy. Nonetheless, the excitement and drama of aviation in the late 1920s and early 1930s often overshadowed the dangers and discomforts. The new airline operators became aware that additional sources of revenue could be gained for the airline industry by winning the public over to this new mode of transportation.

In 1928, one of the four predecessors of United Airlines (UAL), Boeing Air Transport, introduced the twelve-passenger Boeing 80 trimotor. At that time, advertising made modest claims of comforts aloft, although most passengers were still very apprehensive and often airsick, and wives' fears of having their husbands flying still kept many potential travelers earthbound. Extremely conscious of the public's fear of flying during the airlines' formative period, the new airline officials needed promotion of inflight service that would project an image of stability, safety, and comfort to the traveling public. Passenger business, never heavy, fell off more after the Wall Street crash of 1929, and the few airline passengers often needed more care inflight than the copilot was able to provide.

It was in this developmental period of the airlines that Ellen Church, the first female crew member for a commercial airline, entered the aviation industry—not as a copilot, as she had dreamed, but as the first airline stewardess. In cooperation with her company interviewer, Steve A. Stimpson, the San Francisco district manager for BAT, Ellen Church helped formulate the ideas for a new occupation for women on airplanes that would be acceptable to both BAT and the public.

Steve Stimpson had flown as a passenger from Chicago to San Francisco in early 1930, and en route he found that much of his time had been spent meeting the inflight needs of his fellow passengers. As soon as he arrived in San Francisco, he wrote his employers in Seattle urging the addition of a cabin attendant, possibly a Filipino boy, to the flight crew. Given the go-ahead, Stimpson had already hired three male "couriers" when Ellen Church visited his offices on February 23, 1930. Afterward, Stimpson presented BAT with a different and even more novel idea—the possibility of using women in lieu of stewards.[13]

Varying accounts about who conceived the idea of stewardessing reinforce a little publicized fact that Ellen Church, the first stewardess, had thoughts of using her flying skills to become a commercial airline pilot. Stimpson affirmed that "she did have some thoughts of becoming a copilot, but we agreed that it would be better to try to sell Boeing on the idea of women as stewards."[14]

Mary O'Connor, a stewardess with UAL from 1933 to 1961, was personally acquainted with both Church and Stimpson. She believes that Stimpson had already thought about stewardessing when Ellen Church visited the BAT office, and during the interview, Stimpson persuaded Church to round up several acceptable nurse candidates for the possibility of a new flying job.[15]

In its subsidized histories since 1951, UAL has two similar accounts of Ellen Church's pilot ambitions. An Iowa girl who had trained as a nurse in Minnesota, Church had yearned to fly ever since, as a youngster, she had seen Ruth Law, the first woman stunt flier, perform at an Iowa county fair. Ellen Church had taken some flying lessons, but realizing that opportunities for women as fliers were limited, she proposed to Stimpson that BAT hire young nurses as attendants.[16] By 1967, the corporate historical treatment of Church had been revised to describe her as an earnest young nurse from French Hospital, San Francisco, with big dreams about becoming an airline pilot, but after some flying lessons she had realized that flying an airliner was a man's job.[17] Ellen Church may not have disagreed with the notion that flying an airliner was a man's job; however, she did exhibit savvy in making inroads for women within the pioneering airline industry, which manipulated masculine symbols that were so blatantly a part of aviation.

In any case, Boeing Air Transport was not to be the pioneer in 1930 for women commercial pilots in the United States. That distinction was incorrectly claimed by Frontier Airlines, which, more than four decades later, hired Emily Howell on February 6, 1973. Central Airlines employed Helen Richey as a commercial female pilot in 1934; however, she resigned after being rejected by the pilot union, which restricted her to being a "fair weather pilot."[18] United Airlines, the successor of BAT and Central Airlines would graduate its first woman pilot on March 10, 1978.

Stumping the halls of San Francisco and Chicago hospitals, Ellen Church found that the first eight or ten stewardesses had to be sold on the idea.[19] Meanwhile, Stimpson was having difficulties persuading the BAT officials to consider the merits of a woman steward experiment. When his plan was rejected by immediate BAT superiors, Stimpson sought to convince the young, new assistant to the BAT president, W. A. Patterson, of the special value of a stewardess occupation. A standby telegram to Patterson from Stimpson included the following statement: "It strikes me that there would be a great psychological punch to having young women stewardesses or couriers or whatever you want to call them, and I am certain that there are some mighty good ones available."[20] He pointed out that he had in mind a couple of graduate nurses who would make exceptional stewardesses. It would also be understood that no reference need be made to their hospital training or nursing experience, but this would be fine to hold in reserve for airsickness.

Stimpson's follow-up letter also stressed persuasive reasons for hiring these professional women, including the national publicity BAT could get; the beneficial educational experience the qualified applicants would be required to have; and the neater and nicer method of serving food and of looking out for passengers' welfare.

However good Stimpson's intentions may have been, his telegrams reflect a pattern of utilization of female labor in the United States in which demand for cheap, educated labor tended to promote reliance on women in certain occupations. Undoubtedly in 1930 the stewardess concept offered the airline industry many benefits. Even so, Stimpson's enthusiasm for "sky girls," as they were originally called, was not shared by the male hierarchy of BAT's headquarters. Phil Johnson, BAT president, was cool to the idea, and pilots claimed that they were too busy flying to look after a helpless female in the crew.

The decision for the stewardess experiment was left to Patterson, who took the Stimpson memo home in his pocket and after dinner asked his wife to read it. Vera Patterson thought that it was an excellent idea, and the next day Patterson sought to convince his fellow BAT managers "to give this a try."[21] In a major decision that would affect the entire airline industry, Patterson designated Stimpson and Church to hire, train, and put into service eight stewardesses on the Chicago–San Francisco route for a three-month trial period.

Opposition to the stewardess experiment came even before the women climbed aboard for their first flights. Edward V. Rickenbacker, arch-conservative vice president of General Motors with a World War I warbird reputation and the presidency of Eastern Airlines in his future, was vehemently against women working on airplanes in any capacity. Feeling strongly about the issue, Rickenbacker flew from Miami to San Francisco to try to talk Stimpson out of the stewardess idea. He admonished Stimpson, "If you are going to put anyone aboard, stick with the men."[22] His opinions were unheeded, and BAT proceeded with the plan. On May 15, 1930, at 8:00 A.M. at the Oakland, California, airport, a Boeing trimotor plane warmed up to begin a cross-country hop to Chicago with Ellen Church, as the world's first stewardess, aboard.[23]

Specifications for stewardesses drawn up in 1930 called for nurses, not over twenty-five years of age, weighing 115 pounds or less, and not over five feet four inches tall. Pay was $125 per month for 100 hours of flying. Church and Stimpson designed the first uniform under orders from Patterson that "we don't want a bunch of usherettes in pantaloons," and he added that the nurses should not weigh more than 115 pounds in their "scanties."[24] The original eight were Ellen Church, Ellis Crawford, Margaret Arnott, Harriet Fry, Jessie Carter, Cornelia Peterson, Alva Johnson, and Inez Keller. All wore their nurse uniforms during flights in 1930, and changed to uniforms of forest green wool twill suits with capes and berets for ground duty. Creating a no-nonsense image, the original eight uniforms were in keeping with Stimpson's assertion that "I am not suggesting at all the flapper type of girl."[25]

When the eight women began as sky girls, there were few precedents for the job and no more specific instruction than "to make yourself

10

useful."[26] One forerunner of the stewardesses was Albert Hofe, the world's first airline steward, who was hired by the German airline Deutsche Lufthansa in early 1928. Having previously worked for a railroad, Hofe now served hot meals on the three-engine Junkers G-31, which carried fifteen passengers.[27] American carriers, including Western Air and Pan American, also hired couriers and stewards during that year. The couriers hired by Western seemed to be primarily concerned with inflight passenger comfort, but the stewards hired by Caribbean, Eastern, and Pan American worked with docking and mooring airplanes, as well as loading baggage and heavy equipment.

Jessie Carter, one of the original eight stewardesses, quit after three months. She thought it was not an exciting job, and recalled that she was in the air most of the time, flying about a hundred hours a month for $125, and that her ears bothered her. She likened her work to "going cross country on the stage coach."[28] Inez Keller Fruite quit after about four months. She flew the Boeing trimotor the 950 miles between Oakland and Cheyenne, Wyoming, with five stops, and she states that although it was supposed to take eighteen hours, it usually took twenty-four. The planes flew at a height of two thousand feet, and they were not heated, pressurized, or air-conditioned. The food served was the same any time of the day—coffee or tea, fruit cocktail, fried chicken, and rolls. The first stewardesses reassured apprehensive passengers and answered numerous questions about the terrain below. They assisted in unusual tasks, at times joining bucket brigades to help fuel the airplanes or helping pilots push planes into hangars, and they carried all the baggage on board. Stewardesses had to keep a watchful eye on passengers to make sure they did not mistake the exit door for the lavatory door and step into the blue. If all twelve passenger seats were occupied, the stewardess sat on a mailbag or suitcase in the rear of the airplane.[29]

Passengers took almost immediately to the idea of stewardesses on airplanes. Ellen Church was deluged with applications from nurses, teachers, and others, both male and female, who wanted to fly in the new vocation.[30] Still, the employment of women to fly the nation's air routes was a radical concept to some people, and hostilities to the idea emerged. Toleration of the stewardess concept by the pilots came very slowly. The men who retained strong identification with the pilot mys-

11

tique displayed antagonism toward the invading females.[31] During her first week of flying, Church noticed a passenger in acute distress. She told the captain she suspected that the passenger was suffering from appendicitis and was rebuffed with "A guy gets a stomach ache . . . and just because there's a stewardess aboard he raises the roof. . . . Now beat it!"[32] Church was firm and reminded the captain that she was a registered nurse; the pilots reluctantly made an unscheduled stop. Church's diagnosis was correct, and the pilot apologized.

Mary O'Connor, stewardess trainee in 1933, recalled that when she went to Kansas City to get her instructions, she tried with no success to impress the copilots who were responsible for her training with the fact that she was a human being of at least average intelligence.[33]

There were hostilities from other quarters as well. Inez Keller Fruite remembered that wives of the pilots began a letter writing campaign to BAT saying that the stewardesses were trying to steal their husbands and requested their removal. One jealous pilot's wife in Salt Lake City always met her husband at the plane.[34] Boeing Air Transport, perhaps in a supportive gesture to jealous pilot wives, by January 1931, had written regulations to warn off stewardesses: "At no time will steward-esses be permitted to carry on conversations with pilots or ground personnel on duty except on business. . . ."[35] Undoubtedly, such cautionary attempts were mere formalities.

Other airlines were slow in following United's lead in the sky girl experiment. No other U.S. airline commenced this risky experiment until 1933 when American added women to their cabin crews; adding women to their flight crews the same year, Air France has claimed to be the first of the foreign carriers to do so. Somewhat reluctantly, TWA added "hostesses" in 1935 in order to remain competitive. An official with TWA has explained that "United was getting the business." TWA had solicited passenger preference, and 70 percent of the passengers responding said that they preferred the existing setup of having copilots take care of their needs, but "they took to flying United."[36] The TWA official's recollection is somewhat different from another account of TWA's decision to add "stews." In 1935, a TWA DC-2 slammed into the ground in a crash that included some survivors. It became apparent in the postcrash investigations that there might have been more survivors if the plane had carried a cabin attendant. Before the year was out, TWA graduated its first class of stewardesses, copying United by using young women to provide for the safety as well as the comfort of passengers. [37]

Undermining all the arguments against women on airplanes were the business considerations of Stimpson's "psychological punch." It would be difficult for potential travelers to admit fears of flying when young women routinely took to the air as part of the inflight crew. Sex- and age-based discrimination commenced.

Four years after the first stewardesses were hired, suddenly but not totally unexpectedly, the airlines were forced to hustle for passenger and cargo business. When the Democratic landslide brought Franklin D. Roosevelt into the presidency in 1933, the airlines were brought under sharp scrutiny by Senator Hugo Black's investigative forays. Senator Black, whose later contributions as a justice of the Supreme Court are considered by some to have influenced American life more than any of his colleagues in modern times, was enraged by the reasons for the nation's hard times. He set out to make the magnates, who may have caused hardships on Americans, explain their roles. Black's focus was to call the nation's attention to holding companies that exploited government franchises.

Under Postmaster General Walter Folger Brown there had been a mysterious meeting with the operators of the nation's airlines that created suspicion that the nation's airways had been divided up among the big four: United, Eastern, Trans World, and American. No notes were kept on these meetings, but Roosevelt was angry at the implications of contract collusion, and he wanted fast action to expose the participants. James Farley, Brown's successor, used an act from 1872 to cancel the contracts, and Roosevelt, on February 9, 1934, ordered the Army Air Corps to carry the mail in this emergency.

Taking on this enormous task in the middle of the winter, the air corps had neither the modern airplanes nor the pilot readiness for such an undertaking. Airline pilot predictions came true, and within seventy-eight days the army pilots had fifty-seven accidents and twelve deaths. Media attention to these tragic events brought public outrage, and the mail was returned to the commercial airlines. There were stipulations, however. No airline could be awarded a mail contract if it had been represented at the infamous Spoils Conference of 1930. The airlines met this requirement with cosmetic changes of their names. American Airways became American Airlines; Eastern Air Transport was dubbed Eastern Airlines; and Transcontinental and Western Air temporarily added *Incorporated* to its name. United Airlines did not even have to change its name because previous contracts had been awarded to its subsidiaries.

The officials of the airlines who had attended the Spoils Conference were banned from holding airline industry jobs for a period of five years; thus, several airlines were headed by new presidents. It was during this upheaval that W. A. Patterson moved into the presidency of United Airlines, a position he would hold for more than thirty years. Described as honest, fair, and righteous, Patterson initiated a prolonged suit against the federal government to prove that the government was unjustified in canceling the airmail contracts. The United States Court of Claims finally ruled in 1942 that the government was justified.

New Deal legislation was not thrust upon the nation's airlines in the 1930s; it was actively solicited by the industry itself in open demands for regulation from the federal government. Badly hurting from the reduction in subsidies (in 1934 airline subsidies were reduced from $13.4 million to $8 million), the airlines needed the government's help in making the transition to passenger transport; in fact, they needed protection from some forms of unbridled competition among themselves. They also needed a more formalized crash investigation procedure. But perhaps most of all, they wanted stability in maintenance of routes. Under the competitive bidding for airmail contracts, private investment was drying up. Even though Roosevelt preferred placing aviation under the Interstate Commerce Commission, legislative relief came under the Civil Aeronautics Act of 1938. The New Dealers cannot be credited with the act, which was framed to promote "the development of a commercial air transportation system to meet the needs of the foreign and domestic commerce in the United States, of the postal service and of national defense."[38] The act was to remain essentially unchanged for forty years.[39]

The Civil Aeronautics Board (CAB), created by the act in 1940, had wide-ranging authority over air transportation. The method of competitive bidding was replaced by the CAB's ability to issue certificates to the air carriers "of public convenience and necessity." The effectiveness of the CAB was immediately evident. By 1939 the airlines chalked up their first profitable year since the air mail crisis in 1934, and, more important, by 1940 the airlines completed their first year without an accident.

The long, arduous flights worked by United's first stewardesses took their toll. None were still flying in 1936 when the Douglas DC-3 made its debut. The well-designed DC-3 was the first of what has been described as the four major rounds of aircraft innovations.[40] The DC-3 cruised at 180 miles an hour, carried twenty-one to twenty-seven passengers, depending on its configuration, and could fly coast-to-coast with only four or five stops. More than thirteen thousand civil and military DC-3s rolled off the production lines within a decade, the most prolific production ever of any plane.[41]

After the introduction of the DC-3 the stewardess job began to take on permanency. In 1938, United Airlines opened a training center in Chicago for stewardesses, and as early as 1936, American Airlines held training classes in a large room of the Picadilly Hotel in Chicago. American also provided on-site training in hangars at the municipal airport, in the cabins of the "giant transports" inflight, and at catering kitchens.

The stewardess job had changed considerably by the early 1940s. The public accepted the DC-3 as a superior means of travel, and business was on the increase. On a routine American Airlines flight from Chicago to Cincinnati, a stewardess would serve twenty-one passengers a five-course dinner in little more than an hour. She had all trays and debris out of sight before landing, and she had accomplished this feat from a corner measuring three feet by four feet. Her tasks were similar to the approximately one thousand other stewardesses employed by the United States airlines in 1941. At American, the women earned $110 a month for 115 hours of work, of which around 85 hours were flight time.[42]

15

With the arrival of the DC-3s, United Airlines hired hotel man Don Magarrell, who had set up kitchens on the United States Line's S.S. *Leviathan,* to adapt airplanes for food service. Magarrell set up the first flight kitchens for UAL and designed a standard tray with cardboard inserts of the type that have served air travelers ever since. On United Airlines' DC-3s, hot food was padded in insulated boxes and boarded separately from the trays, and soup jugs were used for hot and cold beverages. The only drinking water supply was boarded in two-quart jugs, necessitating conservation of water.[43]

Edith Lauterbach, who worked the DC-3 as a UAL stewardess, could rely on the captain's or the copilot's help in lifting and serving trays. Many UAL pilots seemed to like this break from their flight deck duties and would sometimes argue about "whose turn it was to help the stewardess serve the meals."[44]

The workload of the stewardesses, along with many Americans, increased during the impending war effort of the early 1940s. Air travelers swamped the nation's busy and inadequate airports, standing by for the efficient DC-3 workhorses to relocate them. Many stewardesses found that they were in the air or resting to fly again most of the time. The DC-3 had become their second home. They often exceeded a hundred hours of monthly flight time, compared to today's flight attendant average of 73 hours a month on United Airlines. There was little relief, and after World War II the volume of air traffic continued to boom; the airlines were unprepared for the continuing and sometimes unrelenting demand for aircraft space.

The introduction of four-engine propeller equipment in the postwar years was round two of aircraft innovations. For many airline officials and employees the larger propeller aircraft came not a minute too soon. These airplanes, including the Lockheed Constellation and DC-6, resulted from pressures for larger capacities than the DC-3 and DC-4 could provide. The DC-6, first added to UAL's fleet in 1947, could carry fifty-eight passengers up to 2,520 miles at a cruise speed of three hundred miles an hour.

The large propeller airplanes dominated the commercial air routes throughout the 1950s, and the impression they made with many airline employees and many among the traveling public has never been rivaled. United's inflight services on the spacious and comfortable DC-6 included french pastries, finger sandwiches, elegantly prepared entrees, and moderate servings of the favorite before-dinner drinks. Working as flying partners, two stewardesses now staffed the DC-6 planes for UAL. With the advent of the DC-6, the stewardesses could work within the environment of a pressurized cabin, where administering oxygen became unnecessary except for first-aid purposes. In unpressurized aircraft, the stewardesses flying over the Rocky Mountains had often been required to eliminate inflight services and take oxygen themselves.

Round three of aircraft innovations came screeching in. The industry's swift conversion from piston to turbojet airplanes—for instance, the DC-8 delivered in 1959, which carried 122 passengers at 530 miles an hour up to 3,680 miles—left some flight attendants reeling. The work rules governing the flight attendant's transition from the more leisurely piston aircraft to the jet-propelled airplanes lagged behind the industry's adoption of the new equipment.

Round four, still in progress, began in 1970 with the wide-bodied jumbo jets. The huge Boeing 747, cruising at six hundred miles an hour, can carry five hundred passengers six thousand miles nonstop. [45] On this plane, the flight attendant is part of a crew that numbers from eight to fifteen, necessitating various team approaches for accomplishing tasks.

Accompanying the swift technological changes in commercial aviation were changes in the safety regulations concerning flight attendants. The Civil Aeronautics Administration (CAA), created in the early 1940s, was to have the responsibilities for maintenance of the airways and implementation of the safety regulations established by the CAB. Early in the formation of government regulations regarding air safety the flight attendant had been the forgotten crew member, but the CAA was the agency the cabin attendants hoped would promulgate safety standards through Civil Aeronautics Regulations (CARs). More than a decade after the CAA was created, a modest proposal for a CAR covering cabin attendants appeared:

> One or more competent cabin attendants commensurate with the number of passengers carried, shall be provided by the air carrier on

all flights carrying passengers in aircraft of more than 12,500 lbs. maximum certificated take-off weight.[46]

Victor J. Herbert, acting president of the Air Line Stewards and Stewardesses Association (ALSSA), which represented nearly all of the nation's flight attendants in 1951, argued that the proposal fell far short of the union's expectations of the CAA, and he urged the CAA to go further to include specific regulations for cabin attendant safety duties. Herbert pointed out that the flight attendants' work in crashes is as arduous, demanding, and dangerous as tasks performed by other flight crew members, i.e., pilots. To support his point Herbert cited four incidents that occurred between January 1951 and March 1951 in which the cabin attendants made or could have made a difference in saving lives; in one incident there was no cabin attendant aboard the airplane.[47]

In 1952, the CAA approved the first Civil Air Regulation (40.265) for flight attendants. All air carriers transporting passengers in planes with a capacity for ten or more would be required to provide at least one flight attendant. For thirty years after the first modest cabin attendant crew complement regulations were approved by the CAA, the unions representing flight attendants would appoint safety representatives, collect data on flight attendant safety needs, and testify before congressional committees in a slow evolution of the federal requirements for flight attendants. By 1974 the Federal Air Regulations (FARs) required, basically, one flight attendant for every fifty passenger seats on an aircraft.

With the airlines' greater emphasis on passenger travel in the mid-1930s, the role of airline stewardesses took on new economic importance. During this period, UAL initiated a restrictive and discriminatory requirement as a condition for employment as a stewardess: the women in that position had to be unmarried. The no-marriage rule applied only to stewardesses and not to any other persons employed by United.

As other U.S. airlines began hiring women after UAL's lead, they too adopted the no-marriage rule. There were minor differences. Curiously, American Airlines, as late as 1938 still permitted a woman to continue on the job if she married "provided her marriage will not interfere with her work." If a transfer should arise, she had to accept it or be automatically released; also, American laid off married stewardesses first in the event of a reduction of personnel, which sometimes happened in the lean winter months.[48] UAL Hawaiian male stewards, hired in 1949, were permitted to marry, to have families, and still retain their jobs, and other U.S. airlines that hired male flight attendants, including Eastern and Pan American, did not apply the no-marriage rule to those male employees.

It is questionable if an accurate history of the origins of the no-marriage rule for stewardesses can ever be written. No high-ranking airline official has ever come forward to say, "It was my decision"; and the courtroom rhetoric that emerged from the fair employment practice cases stemming from Title VII of the Civil Rights Act of 1964, has thrown little light on the origins of the no-marriage policy. Lawyers preparing defenses for the airlines have often tried to explain the necessity of the no-marriage rule by tying it to "administrative" difficulties. The legal defense for UAL is fairly typical of several carriers facing similar charges: "The rule was founded on the belief that the irregularity and uncertainty inherent in stewardesses work schedules were in conflict with the woman's role in married life and that such a conflict would have an inevitable adverse effect upon her job performance and motivation. This belief, which stemmed from United's own experience with married stewardesses. . . ."[49]

United's experience with married stewardesses had been extremely limited. Before the mid-1930s, when UAL allegedly first applied the no-marriage rule, few if any, stewardesses had married and continued to fly.

The most plausible factual account of the origins of the no-marriage rule traces it to a decision made by W. A. Patterson, who had become United's president in 1934. Recalling the reasons for the no-marriage rule, Patterson explained that the stewardesses had begun to marry and their husbands started calling into the company at all hours to learn the whereabouts of their wives during delays. He put a stop to the administrative problems by applying a no-marriage rule for stewardesses.[50]

This rather whimsical decision does not explain the motives underlying the policy. A male passenger traveling from Boston to San Francisco on United Airlines in the mid-1960s commented that "stewardesses are America's vestal virgins."[51] The passenger's observation perhaps best defines the reasons for the airlines' no-marriage rule. Before their exploitation by marketing departments of the late 1960s, airline stewardesses, especially those with United, did have a status more akin to vestal virgins than might be remembered. Most applicants considered for the job by United came from the upper or middle economic spheres of America. Many of the airline officials responsible for the continuation of the no-marriage policy approved of their daughters becoming airline stewardesses; in fact, Patterson's only daughter became an airline stewardess in the late 1950s. The United stewardesses, as well as most from other carriers, were considered the personal envoys of their respective carriers. UAL traditionally perpetuated the girl-next-door image, which meant a white, middle-class, reasonably refined, young, unmarried lady. Advertising was geared to this all-American girl image in a nice 1950s approach to the sex-sells concept.[52]

For the protection and convenience of stewardesses, United provided lounges at most major airports. These were secured with locked doors and usually off the main floors of hangars or at other UAL facilities. Most were staffed by a matron to look after the rooms and to make up the beds. Men were strictly prohibited from the premises. The women liked the idea of lounges and negotiated for them in 1946; in 1972, however, the lounges were discontinued when men joined UAL's domestic flight attendant ranks. Now one large room with facilities is shared by attendants of both sexes. A "dark room" in the larger domicile cities, such as Chicago and San Francisco, provides recliner chairs.

The vestal virgins of the air were not expected to stay beyond the usual tenure of eighteen months before they found suitable husbands. Retirement plans seemed like a sad joke; they meant that the women hired for the job had not lived up to their marriageable image. The consequences for violation of the rules were well understood: if stewardesses married, they violated the unwritten corporate policy, and they could suffer the consequences. The alternatives for a married stewardess were transfer to a ground job commensurate with her abilities, provided such openings were available, or resignation. She could usually be persuaded to resign under the guise of protecting her personnel record for future employment inquiries—or she could be fired. Marriage was impossible, and if she took a lover, it could and often did mean termination.

Writing in 1967, an arbitrator for the United stewardess system board of adjustment, the highest appeal level for grievances, verified that knowledge of the no-marriage rule permeated the ranks: "This policy was always widely and well known among the stewardesses. Perhaps because of this fact, the Company took no step to establish a procedure to make certain that each individual stewardess knew about this rule, when she was hired as well as thereafter, until at least 1964. . . ."[53]

John R. Hill, now an arbitrator in California, was hired away from the National Labor Relations Board in 1946 by United Airlines to serve as legal counsel to the company from 1946 to 1970. His initial task was to observe the first negotiations for the first contractual agreement for stewardesses in 1946. He asserts that one has to try to understand the social climate of the times within the country and within the airline companies, specifically United Airlines: "My God, it was an honor to be a stewardess!" United had started the profession of stewardessing, and "they were so proud of that."

In 1946, United Airlines was a small company that fostered a strong family attitude among its ten thousand employees. There was a high degree of paternalism, and there was a strong respect for UAL president Patterson. According to Hill, "There was never anyone at United Airlines, from Patterson on down, who thought anything other than you had to have a young, attractive stewardess. If one asked why you did not believe in the no-marriage rule, it would be like asking a devout Catholic 'Why do you not believe in the immaculate conception?'" Trust and faith in the United Airlines' executive officers was almost unquestioned. It was within this setting that the no-marriage rule "came down from the heavens, like it was carved in granite, that the girl had to be single." He adds: "I guess it was kind of stupid in retrospect—you know, the turnover was terribly high."[54]

But Hill points out that from the 1940s to the 1960s, it was not unusual for parents to guide their daughters into universities to enhance the possibilities of their making good marriage matches. The woman could find a man of means or potential earning power to provide for her. A woman who was successful in the venture would not have to work outside the home, and she could enjoy a degree of derived status from her husband's position. During the decades of the no-marriage rule, the job of stewardessing was also viewed as an acceptable situation that would provide the opportunity to meet advantaged, marriageable men. This idea may have been shared by some stewardess aspirants, but open admission of such within the present ranks of flight attendants is almost guaranteed a laugh. "Today I may meet him!" Marge McCall, a flight attendant with United Airlines, is apt to say as she heads out to work on a plane. When McCall is invited out by passengers she often shocks, angers, or delights the men by asking, "What about mom and the kiddies?"

Throughout the decades of the no-marriage rule, United maintained no policy whatsoever for the pregnant unwed stewardess. An unwed mother remained a disgrace at most levels of American society. Any procedures to cover this embarrassing situation were undertaken by the local domicile management. If she wanted to continue as a stewardess, the pregnant stewardess had limited options: she could obtain an illegal abortion, or, she could deliver and put the baby up for adoption. Mary O'Connor, chief stewardess in Chicago in the early 1940s explained the difficulty of helping pregnant women: "They usually came in because they had no one to talk to. They could not go to their parents, and they often had become pregnant by a married man. As chief stewardess I could give them a leave of absence. I did not approve of abortion. If they did get an abortion that was their decision, and then I would help them if they needed help. I took three or four stewardesses home to my apartment after they had abortions so that they could recuperate. My roommates were very understanding. It was something that no one talked about. . . ."[55] No statistics were kept by UAL on the number of pregnancies that were unofficially processed. UAL continued to hire women of childbearing age and required them to remain single as a condition for the job.

Other, more subtly discriminatory unofficial policies were applied to some early stewardesses. Mary O'Connor's story is an account of such company practices. She was an outstanding stewardess, sought out and rewarded for her successes. She held the job of chief stewardess in

Chicago, served as a nurse for the navy during World War II with the elite Navy Evacuation Corps, and wrote a book for high school aspirants for the job of stewardess, which was published in 1961. She became the first stewardess flight instructor in American aviation in 1940 for UAL, wrote a stewardess manual in 1946, and became the senior stewardess in charge of United's executive airplane, christened the *Mainliner O'Connor* (the first United Airlines aircraft named for a person), in 1946. O'Connor recalled the company's offer for a new training position in 1940: "Would I undertake the training job? Generously they said I'd been a good stewardess and that they did not think the girls would resent having me as that most hated being among girls, a woman boss. Would I try it? . . . Frankly it was an experiment, and it might not work out. . . . I was to remember, however, that should it fail there would be no returning to the rank of stewardess."[56]

It was naive on the manager's part to think that the women would resent a woman boss. Nurses—and all UAL stewardesses in 1940 were nurses—had long experience with female management. Ellen Church had been the first supervisor for stewardesses, and traditionally the chief stewardess was in charge of managing local domiciles for stewardesses. Few groups of working women could have been better acquainted with female management. O'Connor's ability to train was recognized. Once her male manager called her in to ask if it would bother her if a chief stewardess from San Francisco was brought into Chicago to be over her. O'Connor replied, "Yes, it would bother me. I would like to be chief stewardess." The manager explained that the chief stewardess should be photogenic and that she was not photogenic. The manager reassured O'Connor that her job as instructor was more important than the chief stewardess job and that she would continue to make more money.[57]

The working conditions set up by Church and Stimpson continued to deteriorate. In the late 1930s, still being hired to fly 100 hours for $125, the stewardesses found that they often flew up to 160 hours a month. In an innocent move, several women got together at their stewardess layover hotel and compiled a list of grievances. Five stewardesses were chosen to present the signed petition to the company. The company retaliated by threatening to fire the "girls." Some company officials believed that they were organizing a union. Surprised that the company thought this, the stewardesses quickly prepared another petition claiming that the company was treating the five unfairly and gave assurances that they were not unionizing.

While most of the women themselves found any idea of unionizing shocking, the organizing of pilots was well underway. Led by David L. Behncke, a pilot with United Airlines, the Air Line Pilots Association (ALPA) had been formed in 1931. Interest in the pilots' union quickened in 1933 when five major airlines announced that they were going to change the methods of pilot pay, reducing compensation while in some cases simultaneously increasing pilot work. With the temporary cancellation of airmail contracts in 1934, most laid off employees. It was the economic squeeze during these hard times that gave impetus to pilot unionization. Many of the approximately seven hundred pilots in the United States became aware that they were as vulnerable as more ordinary workers to job loss. Nonetheless, the unionization of the pilots was not inevitable, and ALPA's success in mobilizing highly individualistic white-collar workers is significant. [58]

Coming from white, middle-class professional families, stewardesses generally considered themselves to be elite temporary workers or, at the very least, white-collar workers. The job was viewed as a short-term position for women to enjoy before being married to raise a family. Regardless of motivations, the no-marriage rule ensured the company that high attrition would occur within the stewardess ranks.

Although the number of positions had risen from the original eight in 1930 to about three hundred in 1945, United Airlines had in that period hired around fifteen hundred women as sky girls. More than a thousand women had been used as temporary employees during this gradual expansion. [59]

In 1940, the impending effort for World War II made minor modifications in the job of stewardess. Wartime demands for nurses forced the airlines to supplement nurse stewardesses with women educated in other fields. In 1942, half as many planes on UAL carried more passengers more miles than the entire fleet had flown the year before. Due to war priorities, airplanes never flew with an empty seat. Franklin D. Roosevelt planned to nationalize the airline industry much as the railroads had been in World War I, but that threat had been headed off by the airline officials. By pragmatically planning the distribution of aircraft, crews, and know-how, the airlines, acting through the Air Transport Association (ATA), were able to profit handsomely through the war effort, as well as to maintain their status as private enterprise.

Newly hired UAL stewardesses, who faced an increased workload, continued to receive exactly the same base pay the original eight stewardesses had earned in 1930, $125 per month. If a stewardess lasted beyond the initial six months, some provisions were made for modest wage increases based on the recommendation and approval of the stewardess service supervisors: second six months, $140 monthly; second year, $150 monthly; thereafter, an increase of $5 a month until a maximum of $170 was reached.[60]

A union to bargain collectively for wages, hours, and working conditions seemed out of the question. No flight attendant work group had organized in the United States, and unions could readily see that the class and craft possessed conditions that an affiliate would wish to avoid. Low wages of the group would not guarantee essential dues income; UAL flight attendants were all female, and prevailing ideas of female labor groups suggested undependability. Further, stewardesses suffered from forced attrition due to no-marriage rules, which ensured continuing instability of the group. Finally, no government air regulations required cabin attendants to be aboard the nation's commercial aircraft. In a strike situation airlines could train personnel within several days to replace stewardesses, or they could do as Eastern Airlines had done in 1934, dispatch scheduled trips without a cabin attendant.

2
The First Stewardess Union

As the home front participation in World War II began to wind down, some stewardesses felt they were forgotten workers. These feelings intensified when they saw that other workers, especially pilots, had begun to negotiate for higher wages and improved working conditions. The Air Line Pilots Association (ALPA), mainly through its dynamic and colorful leader, David L. Behncke, had accomplished much by influencing federal legislation during the 1930s, in particular the Railway Labor Act. Thus, the future of ALPA as well as the economic position of the pilots had become a matter of national policy. It had been a shrewd and successful strategy to use the contacts on Capitol Hill to solidify political support for pilots and to gain rights for this small but nationally popular group of workers, who numbered only about a thousand in 1937.[1]

The Railway Labor Act (RLA) passed in 1926 primarily as a result of public furor over the disastrous railroad strikes of 1922. Against a background of employer and employee strife that had intensified when the railroads were returned to private operation after federal government management from 1918 through 1920, many managers and union leaders were in agreement that new rules governing the railroads were needed to improve the stability of this essential industry. It was within that spirit of cooperation that the Railway Labor Act was jointly drafted and supported by the railroad industry and its well-established unions. Conversely, the 1936 extension of the Railway Labor Act to air transportation under Title II covered an infant industry where collective bargaining had never taken place.

26

The underlying goal of the act was, and is, to prevent the interruption of service. The act also provides free choice of representation for employees; it allows self-organization of employees with independence from both employers and unions. It provides prompt and orderly settlement of all disputes concerning rates of pay, rules, or working conditions and of grievances.[2]

The impasse resolution provisions of the act are quite brief and somewhat elastic, with much left to the carriers and unions to negotiate; thus, collective bargaining is extremely important. Under the act the National Mediation Board (NMB), composed of three members, who represent both major political parties, is appointed by the president for staggered three-year terms. Aside from the important mediation functions, the NMB handles representation disputes, interprets agreements reached in mediation, and will, upon request, appoint neutral arbitrators for airline grievance cases.

Under the act, employee representation must be by "class or craft" on a carrierwide basis. Signing up potential members of the class and craft is done on a simple card resembling a recipe card, which is entitled "authorization to act." If a majority of employees sign authorization-to-act cards, an election may not be a prerequisite for certification. Voluntary recognition without the NMB certification is permissible and not unusual in the absence of challenge from a rival union. Representatives of the employees need not be in the employ of the carrier. The unions are free to hire people to work for the union members and to represent them to the companies.

The System Board of Adjustment is the only step in the grievance process governed by the Railway Labor Act: the grievance steps that lead up to the System Board of Adjustment are negotiated by the various unions and carriers. The system board is made up of equal numbers of union and company members. An additional member, a neutral arbitrator, is selected either by agreement of both parties, or if no agreement can be reached, appointment by the NMB. A contract administrator (who, for the flight attendants, has historically been a lawyer) presents the case for the grievant, questions witnesses, and makes the arguments. The decision of the majority of the system board members is final and binding.

When the parties to collective bargaining reach an impasse, they may apply to the NMB for mediation. The mediation must be used before the company or the union can resort to "self-help," usually meaning a lockout or strike. Mediation differs sharply under the RLA from bargaining impasses covered by other laws; it has been reluctantly termed "quasi-judicial mediation." The RLA requires much more than mere attendance at mediation sessions. It is the NMB, the government agency under the act, that determines that the best efforts to bring about an amicable settlement through mediation have been unsuccessful. Thus, only in the airline and railway industries must a government agency determine when the parties are released, even in cases not of national importance.[3] The mediator determines how long the sessions continue by his or her power to release the parties or to require continued negotiations.

When the NMB decides that disputes cannot be resolved in mediation, it is required to invite the parties to accept arbitration. Arbitration is usually rejected, and a thirty-day status quo (cooling-off) period goes into effect. Intensive negotiations commonly occur during this period, and if no agreement is reached, the NMB can release the parties. After being released from mediation, the company may change work rules and rates of pay and institute a lockout; the union may decide to accept the company's offer, or it may go on strike. The president of the United States has the ability to appoint an emergency board to investigate the issues if the strike "deprives any part of the country of essential transportation service."[4]

During the early 1930s, some efforts had been made by the pilots' union to bring the airlines under the Railway Labor Act, but company officials balked. It was primarily because of the airlines' anxieties over sharing profits through high salaries to the pilots that ALPA eventually succeeded in bringing the airlines under the act. Title II of the act, written by the pilot union, guaranteed other airline employees the rights and obligations under the act, although the writing of and obtaining support for Title II had been but one aspect of the successful lobbying of and for pilots by ALPA. The pilot union can be credited with much of the rudimentary groundwork for successful labor relations within the airline industry. Before bringing airline employees under the Railway Labor Act, ALPA had experienced jurisdictional problems.

In 1933, when larger and faster aircraft were on the designers' boards, the airlines changed the basis of pilot pay computation from the number of miles and hours flown to a flat hourly pay. Not surprisingly, a dispute followed, and Behncke shopped around for an appropriate government agency to solve this important grievance. On September 21, 1933, ALPA filed with the National Labor Board, charging that the airlines intended to force the pilots into a national strike by means of unreasonable wage cuts. Unintimidated, five major air carriers announced salary changes the following month. With some well-placed phone calls, Behncke persuaded the National Labor Board (NLB) to take jurisdiction of the dispute. NLB Decision No. 83 retained the existing system of hourly rates of pay, rates for day flying, and increases for speeds of more than one hundred miles an hour. This entitled the pilots to share the benefits of future aircraft technology. Nonetheless, it quickly became apparent that no air carrier intended to comply with Decision No. 83, and also that the NLB was unable or unwilling to enforce its decision.

After Decision No. 83, there was renewed interest in bringing airline employees, specifically the pilots, under the Railway Labor Act. Apparently, the airlines' crumbling resistance to the idea was due to a belief that a mandatory application of Decision No. 83 could be eliminated. Thus, Title II of the Railway Labor Act, which brought airlines under the act, was signed with little opposition on April 10, 1936.[5]

Meanwhile, Behncke still had the unresolved problem of making the airlines comply with Decision No. 83, and he was eventually able to implement those provisions by taking yet another avenue. In 1937, at the prodding of the New Dealers, Congress undertook the development of permanent and comprehensive air transport legislation, and it was through the Civil Aeronautics Act of 1938 that ALPA was able to incorporate much of Decision No. 83. That accomplishment, in the face of considerable opposition, was perhaps a zenith for ALPA.

By 1938, the pilots' union was secure, and its success as the first union in the airline industry was to have long-term effects. Most important for airline workers, the spillover effect from ALPA's immediate and successful political efforts in the nation's capital to bring airlines under the Railway Labor Act paved the way for other airline employees to unionize. Sometimes having cajoled, lobbied, and joked politicians into important legislation for airline pilots, Behncke could, by 1939, proceed with collective bargaining under the act with a stance of business unionism.

For reasons that are unclear, by 1941 most airline employees had not followed the pilots' lead to unionize or to exercise their other rights under the Railway Labor Act. Some maintenance workers, primarily mechanics, had organized by 1937 and some dispatchers by 1939.[6] During World War II some communications employees, navigators, and flight engineers formed unions. It has been pointed out that airline jobs were so sought after and held in admiration that some workers, such as United's passenger ticket agents in New York City, were working at "starvation wages" well into the mid-1940s.[7] But, by the mid-1940s, it was dissatisfaction with the most glamorous airline job of all—stewardessing—that came into focus.

In 1944, United stewardesses were white, middle-class, young women who worked for low wages and were forced to resign if they married or had children. Practically no one took the group seriously as a work force. According to a company lawyer of that period, "The stewardess was an important part of our culture. This was not a working woman; this was a glamour job."[8] This attitude was not prevalent within their own ranks, however.

Edith Lauterbach was hired by UAL in 1944. From the outset, while still in stewardess training, Lauterbach questioned the low pay, $125 base salary with no maximum of hours to be flown per month. Indeed, there were no increases in the starting base wage for United stewardesses from 1930 to 1946. Part of that time, from 1941 to 1945, wage and price controls were in full effect in the United States, but nevertheless, wages throughout the rest of the labor force had risen about 40 percent and prices about 22 percent. Lauterbach, along with many of the other 300 UAL stewardesses, had a sincere belief that they, as well as the 10,625 other United employees, had contributed to the World War II effort.[9] In 1941 only about 1,000 flight attendants worked for U.S.

carriers, but by 1947 there were 4,077 stewardesses and stewards in the United States, who represented 4.8 percent of the work force.[10]

Ada J. Brown, a senior stewardess who had four years of flying experience by 1944, was well aware of the reasons for stewardess grievances. She began the movement toward unionization even though she knew of previous attempts in which "girls that had tried to form an association were fired or threatened."

Brown was born in Blackfoot, Idaho, on June 27, 1917, the seventh of nine children. At the age of thirteen, she journeyed to Burlingame, California, to live with her oldest brother and his family. She graduated from Burlingame High School and returned to Twin Falls, Idaho, to work in a small local cafe for a year before entering nurse's training. In 1939, Brown completed her nurse's training at St. Luke's Hospital in San Francisco, and the following year she joined United Airlines as a stewardess. After flying for three years, she became assistant chief stewardess in San Francisco and then advanced to chief stewardess in Portland. For her management positions she was paid from $165 to $195 a month. Ada Brown remembered being frustrated in these positions: "As chief stewardess I tried to get improvements for the girls with salary, flight regulations, and protection from unjust firing. We were always promised things, but nothing was ever done—except to give parties for stewardesses."

On December 16, 1944, after one year as chief stewardess, Brown returned to the rank and file specifically to organize a union. She was advantageously placed to do so because in her management position, she had been "fortunate to have had the confidence of the 'girls,'" and her relations with the company had been cordial. She had taught stewardess classes in Chicago for new hires and therefore had also become acquainted with women in the eastern division.[11]

The movement for stewardess unionization on UAL property was instituted and accomplished completely independently by the women themselves. Brown became the self-appointed organizer at the San Francisco domicile, Sally Thometz at the Denver base, and Frances Hall in the Chicago area. They operated openly in signing up the stewardesses; it is doubtful that a movement could have been kept secret from the company. While the Railway Labor Act granted the women

31

the right to organize, there were other corroborating circumstances at United Airlines's property in 1945. John Hill explained, "An antiunion campaign would have greatly offended United's President Patterson."[12] He believed that within the higher management there was not the slightest antiunion animus. Charles McErlean, retired senior vice president of UAL verified this: "There was no antiunion campaign on United Airlines because we believed it better to deal with a recognized agent. The stewardesses, as short-term employees, especially, would be easier to deal with as a union."[13]

The stewardesses were handicapped by having no precedents for the stewardess class and craft. Sally Thometz, the Denver organizer, told of their initial preparations: "I checked the telephone book, picked out a lawyer, and Ada Brown and I went to his office. I can still see the expression on his face when we asked, 'What is the Railway Labor Act?' "[14] It is not surprising that employees and advisers working with the airlines had difficulties in sorting out the intent of the act. Even today, the act, which is the oldest federal law directly affecting labor and management relations, is probably the least known of all labor legislation. Even among workers covered by the act there is often confusion: in 1981, for instance, a group of United flight attendants dissatisfied with a partnership job-sharing program obtained legal advice and filed their complaint with the National Labor Relations Board (NLRB), which in turn advised the parties that their grievance should be directed to the National Mediation Board under the provisions of the Railway Labor Act.[15]

Meanwhile, obtaining printed authorization-to-act cards, Ada Brown went to work. Within two months she and her inexperienced volunteers had signed up 75 percent of the UAL stewardesses: "No outsider could have organized our group. Even from within our own ranks we had difficulty, although we had the confidence and personal acquaintance of most of the girls. They just did not like the idea of unions. . . ."[16] The organizers were careful to call their union an association. Brown remembers that another difficult organizing problem was keeping up with the high attrition of stewardesses due, in large part, to the company's no-marriage rule. The organizers had to constantly monitor their signature lists and to make sure that they were current. Few, if any, unions have had to cope with the high attrition of workers that occurred in the flight attendant ranks for nearly four decades.

Elections were conducted by the council membership in the four domiciles of San Francisco, Denver, Chicago, and Portland. In turn, the local council officers had elected Ada Brown president of the new national organization, Frances Hall vice president, Sally Watt secretary, and Edith Lauterbach treasurer; shortly thereafter, Sally Thometz was elected conferee (negotiator). All officers had been organizers for the first stewardess union. Concurrently, the women were drawing up a proposed contract to present to UAL and initiating organizing efforts on several other airlines, including Braniff, Continental, and Western Airlines. Interest in the union effort was also building on American, Mid-Continent, and Inland airlines. [17]

The women wrote a constitution and bylaws, a detailed document officially establishing the Air Line Stewardesses Association (ALSA) on August 22, 1945. It ensured a high degree of local autonomy and democracy at the domicile membership level. Brown copied much from the constitution and bylaws of the Air Line Pilots Association. [18]

Throughout the organizing efforts, Brown had sought help and advice from Orvis Nelson, an ALPA officer acting in an unofficial capacity. The pilots' union 1944 convention had passed a resolution to undertake an enormous organizing effort aimed at the various "classes and crafts" within the airline industry. Pointing out that ALPA had written and secured the passage of Title II of the Railway Labor Act, the pilots asserted that it "proved conclusively that their unselfish interest in the welfare of all other workers therein" was clear. In what may well have been a magnanimous overture on the part of ALPA, it resolved to open ALPA's first local council meeting held in 1945 "to other air workers representing groups, or to any person who is interested in organizing such groups. . . ."[19]

From the 1930s on, the pilot union, which was affiliated with the American Federation of Labor (A F of L) had experienced some pressure to organize airline employees. Never anxious to grant large numbers of charters, the A F of L, through President William Green, gave its blessing to ALPA to organize the employees within the airlines under their charter. [20] Already a relatively rich union in 1944, ALPA began a concentrated effort to bring other airline workers under their wing. To finance this undertaking, each pilot (captain) would contribute $15 and each copilot $5 on a voluntary basis.

The new organizational goals of ALPA caused immediate confrontations between Ada Brown and the pilots' association. An official ALPA status report in 1947 explained the organizing blitz and illustrated the origins of the long-lived tensions between the two groups. In it, the ALPA education and organization department acknowledged that the first group to ask for assistance from the pilot union was the stewardesses on United Airlines and went on to say that ALPA agreed to give the women every possible assistance. ALPA provided them with "all essential information and other necessary material," and ALPA representative Karl Ulrich had been assigned to help them with contract negotiations. The terse synopsis then relates that "after further proceedings, the 'girls' failed to follow instructions of the association. Thereafter, ALPA was forced to sever affiliation with them."[21] The implication that Ada Brown and her organizers had been under the pilot union affiliation was incorrect and was later rejected by Ada Brown: "I was never under the employ of ALPA; we were completely on our own."[22] She was, however, seeking advice when she drew attention to the organizing success of the stewardess union in a letter to the pilot union's president David Behncke: "We want this to become a national association. The other airlines are very enthusiastic. We, of course (UAL), wish to become a going concern as soon as possible."[23] Feigning disinterest, Behncke replied, "So far as we are concerned, we must stay in the background and it wouldn't be proper to say that we are your legal representative because we are not. . . . We don't have the authorization to act cards, and, even if we did, it would be questionable because we are another class of employees entirely."[24] Brown had not asked for a legal representative, rather for someone "experienced" in negotiation work to accompany the stewardess representatives to their first negotiation meetings. Without knowing it, Brown was becoming a threat to the pilot union's grand design to unionize the whole range of airline employees.

Brown had moved much faster with organization than the pilot union had anticipated or desired. Behncke and some pilots were displeased that a stewardess union might not be within control of the

ALPA. Forced to continue independently, Brown was disenchanted with the ambivalence of the pilot union's leadership: "Behncke possessed 'Prussian' type characteristics in his personality. He once told me, 'When I say march, march!' Well, I was not going to march for Behncke."[25]

Further, she was convinced that Behncke was ill equipped to advise the first stewardess union. Her conviction may have been well founded. Behncke's professional life had largely excluded women. An adventurous and energetic man, Behncke had run away from his parents' Wisconsin farm when he was thirteen. Three years later, he participated in General Pershing's expedition into Mexico in search of Pancho Villa. He then qualified as an enlisted pilot in World War I and was subsequently rejected twice by the army for a regular commission due to his limited formal education. He worked as a barnstormer and sky advertiser, then flew for Northwest Airlines until he was fired. Finally, he landed a job as a pilot with United Airline's predecessor Boeing Air Transport and commenced his long, successful union career from that position.[26]

The women organizers must have baffled and threatened the pilot leadership. Aside from the garment and textile industries, few U.S. unions had dealt with female membership before World War II. The pilots, considering themselves apart from other working men, certainly must have looked askance as the women moved with efficiency to organize their own group, while showing every intention of running their own union.

Early on, Brown suspected the motives of the pilot union. Victor Herbert, hired by ALPA in 1946 to head the organization for stewardesses and stewards, believed the confrontations between Brown and Behncke were "personality conflicts." Behncke's personality was stamped heavily on ALPA, and partially because of that, Brown did not want to put her newly signed members under control of the pilot union leadership. She also objected to some of the ALPA officers appointed before Herbert.

Brown guarded the authorization-to-act cards signed by stewardesses on United Airlines, the key to union recognition. She recalls, "I needed legal counsel, so I loaded my briefcase with the signature cards and went to Littler [Littler & Coakley], a law firm in San Francisco. I wanted to be sure that it was done properly."[27]

Under the Railway Labor Act, a notice requesting conference dates for the purpose of negotiating an employment agreement on a carrier must be submitted thirty days in advance of negotiations. Brown submitted such a request in August 1945 in the first representation claim on the stewardesses' behalf. The newly formed Association of Air Line Stewardesses (AALS) notified the company that it represented a majority of the stewardesses and desired to negotiate wages, rules, and working conditions. As a result of Brown's letter, United recognized stewardesses as a separate class or craft and was willing to recognize the AALS as the bargaining agent for these employees, provided it could furnish proof of authorization from a majority of the employees in this craft. Brown verified authorization-to-act cards signed by 220 of the 287 stewardesses on UAL's payroll at that time. Shortly thereafter, she submitted the union proposal to negotiate wages, rules, and working conditions for the group. This document also showed that the union had changed its name to Air Line Stewardesses Association (ALSA).[28]

Negotiations for the first stewardess contract began in December 1945 when Ada Brown, Frances Hall, and Sally Thometz met with company negotiators Charles McErlean and E. H. Johnson. UAL needed industrial relations representatives, and United president Patterson had signed McErlean on, sight unseen, to be his adviser of labor relations. By the end of 1945, McErlean called John Hill, a young lawyer who had worked with him with the NLRB during the New Deal years, to come to work at UAL as a legal counsel. Hill was for decades one of the few liberal Democrats within the conservative UAL management. His first job was to attend the first stewardess negotiations as an observer.

Aside from McErlean, Johnson was the only other company negotiator for the stewardess contract, although other company officials, including Roy Wainwright, the superintendant of stewardess service, often sat in on the sessions. Johnson had been an instructor at UAL's training center in Cheyenne, and Hill points out that Johnson had no experience with labor relations, although "he was a kind, sweet man, and he was a genius. He wore thick glasses, nineteen-dollar suits, and rayon socks that showed his ankles."[29] Despite his image, it was Johnson with whom the stewardess negotiators found they liked to deal.[30]

The initial stages of negotiations ran smoothly, although the women experienced some difficulties in establishing their roles. Frances Hall stated, "I believe that the company felt at times, 'Now, this can't be,' that a group of women would be negotiating a contractual agreement in earnest." Hall had the unique experience of negotiating both the first and second agreements, and contrasting the two, she said, "In the second contract, they knew we meant business. They no longer treated us as second-class citizens. We had shown that we were determined."[31] Hill observed, "All men representing the company were chauvinistic. No company, at that time, would have asked a woman to negotiate for the company, so the absence of women was no surprise. It would be like asking 'Why are there no blacks?' No one thought anything about it; it was a way of life."[32]

After commencing in an optimistic and cooperative mood, the negotiations quickly ran into difficulties, then into impasse. McErlean recalled, "The stewardesses thought their contract should be just as the pilots'. Their attitude was, 'This is what we want—give it to us.'"[33] There seemed little room for compromise. For union negotiator Hall, the major point of difference centered around a monthly reduction of flight hours. For the stewardesses, that issue was perhaps the single most important item.

As negotiations dragged on into the early months of 1946, the ALSA women began to run short of money. They did find support from many of the pilot rank and file, especially on United and Western airlines properties, and this assistance was recollected by the first treasurer for ALSA: "When we went to Chicago for our negotiations, we needed more money, but we felt that stewardesses simply could not afford to pay more—and we could not promise them anything. We did receive individual help. Quite often United Airlines pilots would hand me a five-dollar or ten-dollar bill and say, 'Send it to them.' At one time, the UAL pilots based in Salt Lake City took up a collection for our negotiations."[34] It is quite likely that the pilots believed that ALSA was working with their union, so they donated money in the spirit of the 1944 ALPA board of directors' goal to support organization of other airline workers.

It is also possible that in the confusion many stewardesses believed that they had ALPA's support. In fact, the first stewardess union had anticipated ALPA's readiness for an organizational drive for flight attendants by almost a year.

The fledgling ALSA had made provisions for initial membership fees of five dollars, which could be paid on a monthly installment plan. Dues of one dollar monthly were assessed, but as the first stewardesses went into protracted sessions and finally into mediation they were financially strapped. Edith Lauterbach lamented, "We were hanging on, but just barely. We had so little money and we had to try to pay the expenses of the negotiators—it seemed like an eternity to us." She analyzed the company attitude toward the new women's association this way: "UAL management did not believe that stewardesses could organize long enough to negotiate a contract; or, remain organized long enough to renew that first contract."[35]

"The emotional drain was exhausting," Brown said. "We had no one to turn to for help. The other negotiators [Thometz and Hall] were buckling under the pressures, and I had to put up a big front. I couldn't show my anxiousness because I knew it would have a demoralizing effect. One day I broke out in a skin rash—that was one way of letting it come out. . . ."[36]

Although ALSA was on its own, sometime in January 1946, John Hill, as the company observer, heard that ALSA had been guided somewhat by ALPA. Hill believed that it was not because ALPA liked stewardesses, rather the company line had it that ALPA officers knew that the stewardesses would be recognized by somebody and they did not want airline employees under any union inimical to the interests of ALPA. The pilots' interest in a flight attendant union, in Hill's opinion, was more for self-protection of ALPA than for representing stewardesses. His future experience as the company lawyer representing arbitration cases during the next decades would confirm this opinion: "You could tell that they did not have their heart in representing stewardesses."[37]

ALPA had withdrawn moral support and any advisory help to ALSA by March 1946 when negotiations reached an impasse, in part over the issue of limitation of flight hours. Union negotiator Frances Hall considered the low point in the negotiations ALPA's withdrawal of its minimal support of ALSA. The union team wanted the contractual agreement wrapped up without resorting to mediation, because dues were dwindling. The stewardess negotiators had little personal monies to fall back on while negotiating so they returned to their domiciles to fly trips during breaks in the sessions. According to Hall, the company was cooperative in scheduling of meetings, their discussion at those meetings, and their provision of free transportation for union business. It was after ALPA's desertion that the ALSA negotiators renewed their determination to exert themselves as union leaders; they had commenced the machinery under the Railway Labor Act, and they had opened channels through negotiations. "I do not think that 'Brownie' felt intimidated," Hall remembered, "and I was borrowing courage from her."[38]

When negotiations seemed hopelessly deadlocked, Brown was contacted by the company representatives to arrange for an official business luncheon. The company employee that UAL dispatched was a young man whom Brown had never met before. She described him as "one of the most handsome men that I had ever seen," and suspected that she was the object of one of the oldest sexual ploys. More than thirty years later Brown's anger at the incident was tempered with amusement.[39]

One day the stewardesses arrived at a session to state that they were going to ask for mediation from the National Mediation Board under the terms of the Railway Labor Act, but first they wanted to talk with UAL president Patterson. McErlean and Johnson, both being new and never having negotiated a contract before, communicated that request to Patterson with the advice that he deny it. It was considered poor strategy to let the union team make an end run around the company team and go to the head man. But it was characteristic of Patterson to reject the company officials' advice.

The company and union negotiators went into Patterson's office together. Patterson was congenial, causing Hill to believe that the stewardess negotiators made a tactical error when they implied that they were threatening the company by going into mediation. Patterson's response seemed to disappoint the stewardess negotiators: "No, he did not think that was anything to shy away from—he thought that it was a good thing to go into mediation."[40]

Analyzing the results of the meeting as "poor," Ada Brown explained why she and the other negotiators decided to talk to Patterson before requesting mediation. There was a strong belief that Patterson did care about the welfare of employees and that if their problems were brought to his attention he would support and institute changes to correct the situation.[41]

The union requested mediation in March 1946 and on March 19, 1946, a letter from the National Mediation Board advised United that the union's request for mediation services had been docketed as NMB case no. A-2291.[42] Neither the company nor the union negotiators recalled the mediation period with any clarity. The mediation period for the first contract for flight attendants lasted a little more than one month. "The mediator was having trouble," McErlean said, "There was no room for negotiations. The company was now ready to buy a contract, but the company was not going to give them the pilot contract."[43] Mediators have no power of enforcement. Their role is simply to mediate, with no time limits as to how long the talks may continue. These decisions lie with the NMB. The union women and the company representatives stubbornly asserted their roles. It paid off on April 25, 1946, when Ada Brown, Sally Thometz, and Frances Hall signed a contractual agreement for ALSA along with W. A. Patterson, Charles McErlean, and E. H. Johnson for the company. A "voluntary recognition" of the union was accomplished. Although Brown had the necessary signatures on the authorization-to-act cards, the company's "voluntary recognition" of ALSA eliminated the necessity for formal certification by the National Mediation Board. Recognition of most representatives for flight attendants since then has been accomplished by elections conducted under the auspices of NMB. Infrequently, voluntary recognition has also been granted. Without a union of their own, some flight stewards at Pan American had contractual provisions negotiated by unions that represented other employees, some as early as 1945. The Pan American steward representation had been carved up within divisions of that company, and some attempts were made to include them in negotiated agreements that other workers obtained.[44]

There had been no recognition of any flight attendant union before United's voluntary recognition of ALSA and no certification by the National Mediation Board to any union for representation of flight attendants.

Backdated to be effective January 1, 1946, the agreement was the first contract between an air carrier and the stewardess-steward class and craft in the United States.[45] The first union for women working as stewardesses was now a reality. The goals of ALSA had been to obtain adequate wages, establish flight limitations, and secure better working conditions on the ground as well as in the air. ALSA also negotiated to provide an effective channel for grievances, to protect stewardesses against unfair practices, and to guard against favoritism. Finally, the union's goal was also to elevate the role of the stewardess to a more meaningful level. "We did negotiate for a lot more than we achieved, Frances Hall acknowledged. "But, now, never again could the company say 'you can fly twenty hours or more in a row.' That was over."[46]

Sally Thometz appraised the contract as "not the greatest, but we got one!"[47] But in fact, the first contract made radical changes in the UAL stewardesses' work lives. Raising the beginning salary from $125, which had remained unchanged since the original eight took to the skies in 1930, to $155, the negotiators went on to settle other issues. ALSA bargained relief from the conditions of no uniform allowance, no ground pay, no legalized rest periods, no flying time limitations, and nothing to protect stewardesses from indiscriminate dismissal. As a result, ALSA gained a commitment from the company to pay one-half the costs of the initial uniform, $1.30 an hour for ground time for irregularities (any holding time in excess of one hour during which stewardesses were required to remain with passengers), guaranteed rest periods, and restricted flying time. A stewardess was entitled to a fifteen-minute rest period for every two hours that she was required to hold with passengers on the ground.

Actual flight hours were limited to eighty-five a month with no more than 255 hours within any three consecutive calendar months. A stewardess was not to be scheduled to fly more than eight hours in any twenty-four-hour period, and after a period of duty she was entitled to a rest period of two hours for each flight hour flown. Finally, detailed provisions for representation of ALSA members in grievances and dismissals were written into the agreement.[48]

Another high priority had been gaining the right of stewardesses to inspect their company-held personnel files. It was believed that this provision would help eliminate local domicile managers' arbitrary application of unreasonable discipline. As chief stewardess, Brown had seen evidence that the company had docked the pay of stewardesses as punishment for abuse of UAL regulations, and during the first negotiations Brown is remembered to have called a bluff by reaching for her briefcase to present documents proving her charges.[49] Fortunately, she was not asked to produce this evidence, and the negotiating team was able to secure a provision giving stewardesses access to their personnel files.

The company had made concessions in almost every paragraph of the twenty-eight-page agreement of 1946. Some were small, such as the $30 raise in starting pay, and others, such as legal recognition of the first flight attendant union, significant—a union for stewardesses could henceforth collectively bargain with the company for rates of pay, rules, and working conditions.

The sophistication and detail apparent in the first contract may be traced to the zeal of the pioneering women negotiators, the managerial expertise Ada Brown acquired as chief stewardess, and the labor relations experience and philosophies of the company negotiators, Charles F. McErlean and E. H. Johnson.

Overriding all these factors was the attitude fostered by UAL president Patterson. Using UAL's personnel department to systematize information as early as 1935, when other airlines were still using their personnel departments for hiring and firing, Patterson created a natural basis for the work of industrial relations. Organization on UAL property would not include a hate-the-boss campaign partly because Patterson, although he had shown initial resistance, later moderated his stance and had been broken in with the Air Line Pilots Association during the 1930s.[50] Patterson observed early that fighting ALPA was a no-win proposition. The early pilot union success plus a rudimentary background of industrial relations on UAL enabled a relatively smooth process of unionization for nonmanagement employees. Finally, at

UAL there was corporate conscience about adhering to the intent of laws governing the airline industry, as well as a belief that dealing with unions would be a superior and efficient system of employee relations. Patterson, an industry leader of the times, grasped the significance of working with the growing union movement.

All airlines were undergoing a big change after World War II. The postwar surge in air travel saw United's work force increase from 8,177 employees to 13,939 during 1946. Airline management had underestimated the volume of peacetime travel, which at United rose 25 percent above forecast figures in 1946. A breakdown in efficiency in ground services prompted Patterson to write: "I am not interested in how bad the service of other airlines may be . . . I am comparing United Air Lines' service now with United Air Lines' service of the past," and he pressured UAL's management to deal with these very serious problems.[51] The timing of the stewardess agreement enabled stewardesses to face the growth problems with restrictions on how much work management could require from them.

The union agreement of 1946 had launched a new era for UAL stewardesses and provided the basic formats for contracts the ALSA went on to negotiate for 1947, 1948, and 1949. These agreements all included more specific language regarding working conditions and rules, and the contract of 1948 included a very important item, equipment differential pay. In addition to their base salary, UAL stewardesses now earned incentive pay for hours flown over sixty, sixty-five, and seventy hours, to a maximum of eighty-five hours, depending on the speed of the equipment to which they were assigned. The 1948 agreement also included a copy of government regulations that covered pilots' flight hours. The stewardesses had negotiated this feature to ensure rest and legality restrictions.[52]

Despite contractual gains, the weak financial position of ALSA continued to overshadow any successes. There was never enough money to hold necessary conventions to elect officers, for publication and dissemination of information, or, most important, for legal assistance to process grievances. ALSA was beginning to experience an old, lingering problem familiar to many small unions. Grievance representation, the most important function of unionism, was almost out of reach for

ALSA. Union administration of the contract has to be effective before a union can be considered a serious entity, and in order to react to management interpretations of the contract, ALSA had to activate its grievance machinery.

A crucial financial blow came in 1949 when ALSA actively opposed the company's plan for staffing the new San Francisco–Hawaii routes in 1947. The dispute involved the company's right to arbitrarily reinstitute the pre–World War II nurse qualification requirement to include one nurse per trip on the Hawaiian route. This issue was the substance of ALSA's first grievance to the System Board of Adjustment. [53]

The issue was considered critical by Patterson. He believed that the length of the route made it necessary to have someone on the staff with medical knowledge. John Hill, who researched the case and presented the company's position to the system board, knew that Patterson's idea of reinstituting the nurse requirement was disliked by many within stewardess management. [54] During the 1947 negotiations, the union had objected to plans to add nurses to the operation. The issue had not been settled, and for the next year the company did not add a nurse on the Hawaiian routes. During the 1948 negotiations the issue again came up, and the union representatives said only, "We have our grievance." In June 1948, shortly after the 1948 contractual agreement was signed, the company arbitrarily added a nurse to the operation when a resignation from a nonnurse stewardess occurred.

Advising Hill as he prepared the case for the company, Charles McErlean interpreted the Railway Labor Act as providing for this situation in a rather oblique way. The union, he believed, could have taken this disagreement to the mediation board within a specified period of time. When they failed to do so, the company was free to put the rule into effect. [55]

ALSA hired labor lawyer Roland C. Davis to present its case. The neutral arbitrator for the case, Willard Wirtz, was a law professor and would later become secretary of labor under presidents Kennedy and Johnson. Neither the lawyers nor the arbitrator had ever processed a case under the provisions of the Railway Labor Act. Davis argued the case for the union as if it were a billion-dollar court case rather than a dispute in arbitration. Edith Lauterbach, who was an ALSA witness at the hearing, reported to the membership that "it was a delight to hear the cause of the Association so ably extoled."[56]

For the company, Hill claimed that the union had erred in negotiations in proposing this change in the rules and then not taking the issue to mediation. Hill explained that this had been McErlean's position, and while it seemed rather arcane to him, it turned out to be right. ALSA lost the case.[57]

In his decision, Wirtz pointed out that the parties "had agreed to disagree." The issue had not been settled in collective bargaining, and that was where a conclusive determination of the issue could be reached. Eventually, in 1969 the nurse qualification on Hawaiian routes was negotiated away by the Stewards and Stewardesses Division of ALPA. The change was effective January 1, 1970, and thus, Wirtz's decision permitted UAL to maintain the qualification of registered nurse for twenty-one years.

The case proved the vulnerability of the small, independent stewardess union. Under the Railway Labor Act, the carrier and the union share the costs of the system board. Thus, while it was not an unusual cost, it depleted the union's resources and irreparably weakened ALSA.

It had been the intention of UAL to add a Hawaiian "girl" to the staff of its Pacific flights, but in a turnabout and in its first voluntary exception to the sex requirement for the job of flight attendant, UAL arbitrarily added Hawaiian men to the new Boeing stratocruiser on the Hawaiian routes. That decision reduced the regular stewardess seniority list to one-third of the Boeing stratocruiser crew complement. Unable to challenge the move, the women on the Hawaiian route had to resign themselves to this erosion of seniority rights. The reason usually given for the addition of a male attendant for that route was that the stratocruiser service required the lifting of heavy boxes. "We considered it a joke," Edith Lauterbach recalled, "to use the lifting excuse, because one of the original eight stewards was so small that he had to stand on a box to reach the upper compartments in the galley. Most of us could ably lift him onto the box. . . . On the other hand, the island men were congenial, and the working relationships were generally excellent between stewardesses and the Hawaiian men."[58]

Meanwhile, the group had captured the interest of several national unions, which sensed the readiness for organization of the class and craft of stewardesses. Unable to bring Ada Brown's movement under acceptable control, the ALPA leadership, on August 1, 1946, formed the Air Line Stewards and Stewardesses Association (ALSSA) in direct competition with ALSA. Simultaneously, organizing efforts to bring Pan American World Airways flight attendants under a certified union were underway. These were not going smoothly.

Because Pan Am began hiring women in 1944, most Pan Am flight attendants in 1946 were men. In March and April 1946, under the auspices of the National Mediation Board, the required secret ballots were distributed to the 341 Pan American stewards and stewardesses who were eligible to vote. Options on the ballot included the Transport Workers Union (TWU), affiliated with the CIO, and the Flight Stewards Federal Labor Union, which had represented the Latin American division of Pan Am. When the ballots were counted on April 9, 1946, a majority of Pan Am attendants had not voted.

It is likely that Pan Am wished to have its flight attendants represented by a single union, and on May 23, 1946, a letter of interim recognition, pending clearance of unchecked signatures in the divisions, was sent to TWU by Pan American vice president Franklin Gledhill. On May 27, 1946, the National Mediation Board officially closed the case on the representational election without granting certification. On June 7, 1946, Pan American offered voluntary recognition to the Transport Workers Union and informed the union that the company representatives would be available to begin negotiations, which eventually led to a systemwide bargaining agreement between the company and the stewards and stewardesses. TWU continued to hold representation rights for Pan Am flight attendants for more than thirty years.[59] The International Association of Machinists and Aerospace Workers (IAM), also wanting to get into the act, had attempted unsuccessfully to organize the National Airlines flight attendants.

It was during these times that Ada J. Brown's employment within the airline industry was quickly and permanently severed because she decided to marry. Brown Greenfield unhesitatingly stated, "I would have continued my flying career as a married woman if the policy of the company had permitted me to do so," but in 1947, Brown, at the age of thirty, fell victim to UAL's no-marriage rule.[60] She delivered her farewell address to the ALSA membership. Described as "forty years ahead of her times," part of Brown's prescription for the future of the stewardess union was indeed apt.[61] She pointed out that it was unwise for ALSA to remain independent and that it was essential to have the power that a national union could offer to protect stewardesses in difficult labor-management problems.

The options for affiliation for ALSA were limited. An affiliation through ALPA would cause problems, according to Brown, because as yet ALPA's organization was not a democratic one. Brown had found that ALPA's appointed officers were sometimes without airline experience and always without a knowledge of stewardess work conditions. She believed that the pilots' union would continue to pay lip service while neglecting the stewardesses' needs.

Brown recommended joining Flight Pursers and Stewardesses, a group that had started much as ALSA, and at that time included different groups within the airline industry.[62] Although some union convention accounts have claimed that Brown feared a take-over by the CIO, Brown Greenfield said, "Untrue. We wanted representation, but I did not hold any prejudice against the CIO."[63] Brown's position may have been confused with ALPA's stance against the CIO. As early as May 15, 1947, the pilots issued a statement that their interest in organizing the stewardesses into the Air Line Stewards and Stewardesses Association was to keep out certain other groups, including the CIO, machinists, Teamsters, and some railroad employees' organizations. All these groups were described in the pilots' warning as "angling to organize the stewards and stewardesses."[64]

In 1946, ALPA began an all-out effort to win the representational rights of stewardesses and stewards; by the late 1940s the pilots had organized agents, mechanics, flight engineers, navigators, and other groups, including stewards and stewardesses. Managing to capitalize on Ada Brown's efforts on Mid-Continent, as well as on American Airlines, ALPA took over by means of ALSSA. From 1946 to the mid-1950s, twenty-one elections affecting 3,457 flight attendants were carried out under the National Mediation Board's auspices. Nineteen flight attendant groups gained recognition, and fourteen of the nineteen voted to affiliate through ALSSA with ALPA.[65]

Victor Herbert, who was hired by ALPA in 1946 to organize the stewardesses, had accomplished this assignment with astonishing success. The soft-spoken Herbert was fresh from the navy and had no prior union experience. Herbert, who is now head of the ninety-five hundred members of the Air Line Employees Association (ALEA), comprised mainly of ground employees, explained the success of organizing the Air Line Stewards and Stewardesses Association. First, he had about fifty-five thousand dollars in ALPA funds to accomplish the effort; second, the stewardess group was ripe for organization; and, third, the pilots had a special high status with employers. Riding the coattails of the pilot union greatly enhanced Herbert's efforts to organize flight attendants.[66]

ALSA members, who included the United stewardesses and the Western stewardesses who joined ALSA August 6, 1946, had always maintained a high degree of harmony with the rank-and-file pilots; and on December 2, 1949, ALSA, under its third president, Irene Eastin, merged with the ALSSA. Eastin, now the city manager for Hertz Rent-A-Car corporation in San Francisco, said that there was no resistance from ALSA members to merging with ALSSA: "Those of us who understood ALSA's financial situation knew that we could not remain independent and perform the necessary functions of a union."[67]

Eastin had earned a degree with an emphasis on business from the University of Colorado before she became a stewardess in 1946. Taking over ALSA's presidency from Frances Hall in 1948, she wasted no time in pointing out to the members that ALSA was limited in members, authority, financial resources, and experienced leaders. She explained that ALSA's constitution and bylaws were almost identical to ALSSA's.

When the National Mediation Board tallied the United representational vote on February 24, 1950, the UAL stewardesses officially became ALSSA members. The unforgotten ALSA sisters, so carefully organized by Ada Brown, on Western Airlines joined ALSSA on March 7, 1950.[68] It was brought to UAL president Patterson's attention that the company could have the representational vote checked for accuracy. Patterson's response was "'No, do not check the legalities. The stewardesses need a union.'"[69]

The experiment in independence, a term somewhat contradictory to unionism, was over. But any ideas the pilot union may have had of easily controlling the stewardesses under an affiliation were short-lived. The women began immediate confrontations over affiliation status and over the male leaders of ALSSA appointed by ALPA, and for the next quarter century the pilots and stewardesses would quarrel over the right to self-determination.

Right: The original eight stewardesses, c. 1930. Clockwise from upper left: Ellen Church, Alva Johnson, Jessie Carter, Ellis Crawford, Harriet Fry, Cornelia Peterman, Inez Keller, and Margaret Arnott. (Photo courtesy of United Airlines.)

Facing page, left: Ada Brown and Frances Hall, first negotiators for the flight attendants, during the 1945 negotiations with United Airlines. (Photo courtesy of Association of Flight Attendants.)
Right: Mary O'Connor, first flight attendant instructor, and the aircraft named in her honor, c. 1946. (Photo courtesy of United Airlines.)

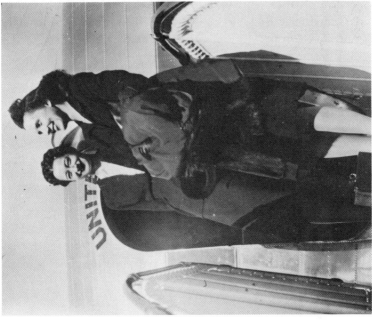

3
An Unequal Partnership

In the early 1950s, the pilots for the nation's commercial airlines could anticipate growing prosperity and security. In sharp contrast, flight attendants looked toward increasingly unsure working conditions on ever larger and faster airplanes. Introduced in 1948, the large, four-engine propeller planes, exemplified by the DC-6, were comfortable and spacious. They were also destined for quick obsolescence. In the spring of 1950, with the commercial jet age less than a decade away, UAL president Patterson sent the airline's best engineering brains to Europe to ride in the new British jet transport planes and appraise their effect on United's fleet in the years immediately ahead.[1]

It is not surprising that pilots often viewed the women who shared their workplace aloft as employees with short-term interests in wages and working conditions. Perhaps at no time in American history had employer discrimination against women been sanctioned by greater social acceptance than in the 1950s. The mystique described by Betty Friedan as a "glorification of woman's role" seems to have reached unusual social acceptance during the immediate postwar years.[2] Stewardesses were limited by the societal trend to narrowly define woman's place as within the home. While women often looked upon the ultimate achievement as an engagement ring with a small solitaire diamond, which would later be interlocked with a matching wedding band, female employment was increasing faster than male employment. Women were entering the workplace in greater numbers than ever before. By 1960, twice as many women were at work as in 1940, and 40 percent of all women over sixteen held a job.[3]

From these often deceivingly quiet years came the cold war, Mc-Carthyism, and the word *un-American*. Millions of American workers were affected by these highly emotional concepts. Union officials initiated housecleaning to root out corruption. Some unions, especially those affiliated with the CIO, were more often targeted as hotbeds of communism than others. In 1952, both the elderly William Green, the head of the A F of L, and Philip Murray, who led the CIO, died. Taking over the A F of L, George Meany vigorously sought a coalition with the CIO, which was under the new leadership of Walter Reuther. The A F of L and the CIO were merged in 1955, and the reconciliation of the many differences that had kept the two groups apart for eighteen years commenced.

In addition to shifts in the nation's mood, changes in legislation also affected stewardess unions. In 1951 the Railway Labor Act was amended to permit the union shop, and the following year the flight attendants secured the first modest civil air regulations to require attendants aboard all U.S. commercial aircraft as cabin safety personnel. During 1958, the airlines entered into a mutual aid pact (MAP), which permitted airlines to share unearned profits in response to a strike against one of them. Each member would pay the struck member carrier all the net income from the strike-diverted traffic. In some instances the MAP provisions would make it profitable for carriers to take strikes. (In 1978, the existing MAP was voided by the Airline Deregulation Act of 1978. While not outlawing the MAP, the act severely limits its use.)

The Labor-Management Reporting and Disclosure Act (LMDRA), known as the Landrum-Griffin Act, was signed in 1959. It contains a bill of rights for union members and requires that a union's constitution and bylaws and information concerning dues and fees be filed with the secretary of labor. Unions must also furnish information about rules that limit member participation or that provide for discipline by fines or expulsion. Company officials and the union representatives of its employees are required to report all direct or indirect personal monetary and business transactions among them. All this information is available to the public.

The Landrum-Griffin Act is pro-American and pro-public in the 1950s style. Restrictions against Communists were written into the statute (section 504a). Communists and some categories of ex-convicts could not hold certain offices in the unions or act as labor consultants for management until five years had passed after leaving the Communist party or other requirements had been satisfied. The unconstitutional aspects of the Landrum-Griffin Act were successfully challenged by, among others, Archie Brown, a long-time worker in the longshoremen's union in San Francisco.[4]

Although some of its provisions were specifically aimed at Communists, the Landrum-Griffin Act also applied to the more conservative unions. ALPA's constitution and bylaws came into conflict with the intent of the act. Restriction of officer candidacy to ALPA members, while not unlawful, had preceded the act. Ada Brown had recognized ALPA's undemocratic elements, and she was among the first to speak out against them.[5] The ALPA policies had been an ongoing concern to the A F of L, and its president, George Meany, frequently urged ALPA to amend its constitution and bylaws to enable the assimilation of other classes of airline employees into the union. Meany stressed that the flight engineers had been issued a federal labor union charter in 1948 "because, and only because, the ALPA would not take this class of employees into membership."[6] He noted later that although the A F of L on many occasions from 1933 on had requested ALPA to take all the air line groups in, "for some ten or fifteen years they did very little. . . ."[7] In matters of its constitution and bylaws ALPA seemed unconcerned about risking the displeasure of the A F of L or later the AFL-CIO.

Joining ALPA's affiliate ALSSA, United stewardesses soon found that some rights held under the independent ALSA were altered. From 1936 to 1942, ALPA's constitution and bylaws contained a clause that was sexist, racist, and typical of A F of L charters at that time. "Any male of the white race, of lawful age and of good moral character, who is legally qualified to serve as a pilot or copilot on aircraft in interstate or foreign commerce, shall be eligible for membership. . . ."[8] Furthermore, under the pilots' union constitution and bylaws the ALPA executive committee was empowered to voluntarily sever affiliations either on a temporary or permanent basis. A conditional charter had been granted to ALSSA by ALPA on November 24, 1947. This charter could be revoked at any time by the all-male ALPA executive committee. Their first contract under ALSSA, signed on September 28, 1950, shows that their president and negotiator, Irene Eastin, had been downgraded to signing the contract as a witness.[9] According to Eastin, there was really little difference in de facto power, and although Victor J. Herbert signed the agreement as the appointed acting president of ALSSA, the actual negotiations and agreement were made by the women themselves.[10]

Nevertheless, the UAL stewardesses could see the potential advantages in their merger with ALSSA. The pilots' organization of cabin attendants had been rapid and impressive. By the time ALSSA had its first convention in June 1951 at the Sherry Hotel in Chicago, the union had become the bargaining representative for approximately thirty-three hundred stewardesses on thirteen trunk airlines and eleven feeder lines and had negotiated more than fifty-five contractual agreements, amendments, supplemental agreements, and other related documents between eighteen airlines and their flight attendants.[11]

During the second day of the convention, June 6, 1951, ALPA granted a regular charter to the stewards and stewardesses,[12] and ALPA's president, David L. Behncke, delivered an extemporaneous speech to the flight attendants and guests. He acknowledged that Victor Herbert had been the force behind the organizing effort and advised that "it would be unwise for the ALSSA organization, at only five years old, to cut loose from ALPA."[13] Although ALPA clearly wanted the stewards and stewardesses to "solo," Herbert would remain assistant to the newly elected officers of ALSSA "as long as ALSSA desired."[14]

Mary Alice Koos, running on the platform of certification for stewards and stewardesses based on uniform standards for safety training and proficiency, was elected the first president of ALSSA. Koos commenced flying as a stewardess for Capital Airlines in 1945, then called Pennsylvania Central Airlines, which granted her a two-year leave after her election. Other officers elected were Joseph Oliver, Eastern Airlines, vice president; Irene Eastin, United Airlines, secretary; and Ruth Schmidt, Trans World Airlines, treasurer. [15]

For a woman to head an international union was, and is, a news-making event. An editorial in ALSSA's publication *Service Aloft* recognized the uniqueness of the female union leader and conceded that women were difficult to organize—at that time out of 18 million women in the labor force, only 3 million were members of unions. It was noted that the *Directory of Labor Unions* for 1951 should contain a big neon marker for the listing of the name of Mary Alice Koos as "she will be the only union president of the female gender."[16] The women of ALSSA, however, accepted female leadership as natural.

Although they possessed modestly comfortable assets of forty-one thousand dollars, ALSSA was still indebted to the pilots' union for earlier financial aid, and ALSSA's appointed officers were being paid by ALPA. Noting that the approximately fifteen hundred dues-paying ALSSA members were carrying the burden of negotiation and arbitration for the thirty-three hundred flight attendants represented by the union, the delegates voted to direct negotiators to include provisions for a union shop in all ALSSA employment agreements. A union shop would require all flight attendants to become dues-paying members. In a most important mandate, the convention delegates voted to seek affiliation with the A F of L on an independent basis, separate from ALPA.[17]

There were three major differences in the ALSSA convention mandates and the pilots' goals for the group. First, the women approved of certification of their occupation, which would be similar to the licensing of pilots; ALPA disapproved of that measure for flight attendants. Second, ALSSA wanted the union shop, which would require all flight attendants to become dues-paying union members; at that time ALPA was opposed to union shop, claiming that if a union makes itself attractive potential members will join automatically. Third, ALSSA delegates directed their officers to request their own independent charter from the A F of L. Such a straightforward stand for independence by the first flight attendant union delegates presented an awkward and disconcerting problem to both ALPA and the A F of L.

On the issues of certification and union shop, ALPA took no public position, but within the union opposed these measures. ALPA officers' early concern about federal licensing of stewards and stewardesses was that if these "ticketed girls" went on strike they could not easily be replaced by scabs,[18] and in more recent years pilots expressed concern that licensing of flight attendants might interfere with the concept of one authority—vested in the captain—on the aircraft.[19] Flight attendants in the United States have not yet obtained certification or licensing from the applicable government agencies.

The stewardesses were at philosophical odds with the pilots over the union or agency shop concepts. In an agency shop, all employees in the bargaining unit who do not choose to join the union are required to pay a fixed amount monthly, usually the equivalent of union dues. In a union shop, all employees are required to become members of the union within a specified time after being hired, and they must remain members of the union as a condition of continued employment. For administration of a union or agency shop agreement, a dues checkoff arrangement is often negotiated whereby the company may automatically deduct dues from the employee's salary and submit the sum to the union. The checkoff is preferred by many members so they do not have to make payments to the union.

ALSSA had not been making money or even breaking even under ALPA. With fewer than 50 percent of the flight attendants paying dues, the pilots often had to compensate for the deficits of the stewardess organization. ALPA therefore kept its opposition to the union shop low-key. Victor Herbert, acting president of ALSSA from 1946 to 1951, recalled, "I have always been for union shop; I have never supported ALPA's position on this issue."[20]

A serious threat to the relationship between the flight attendants and the pilots was implied by the mandate from ALSSA delegates to acquire a charter through the A F of L. In compliance with this convention directive, ALSSA filed its first application for a charter with the A F of L in June 1951. Four months later, the charter application was withdrawn by an unknown ALPA employee without the knowledge or consent of the officers of ALSSA.[21] The application for the charter must have embarrassed the A F of L because the A F of L had pressured ALPA to take in the stewardesses and stewards along with other airline employees. The pilot union continued to publicly encourage and privately discourage the flight attendants' drive for their own charter as ALSSA reapplied in 1954, 1957, and 1959 for an international charter (the 1957 and 1959 applications were made to the AFL-CIO).

For two years after the 1951 convention, ALSSA was still under the supervision of ALPA. Victor Herbert, as ALPA's liaison, stayed on as an adviser and watchdog for the women's union. His title was downgraded to assistant to the president, but he was empowered to override decisions made by the ALSSA president. Because Koos was so capable, Herbert never found it necessary to use this power.[22]

Although the flight attendants had control over their own negotiations at each property, Koos assisted the various teams with the bargaining. She used ALPA's staff for legal assistance, and at times ALPA negotiators as well. The short contractual agreements, which ran from one to one and one-half years and were typical at that time, kept negotiations for many carriers open on a continuing basis. While the group was negotiating on several properties, they would be simultaneously preparing openers or proposals for other carriers.

Koos ran up against company proposals to negotiate mandatory retirement for stewardesses, usually at the age of thirty-two or thirty-five. She recalled that the companies employing stewards, including Eastern, Northwest, and TWA, did not propose early retirement for men. ALSSA vehemently opposed such discriminatory early retirements. Koos was proud of the fact that ALSSA did not negotiate a single contractual agreement with that discriminatory provision during her presidency, although company pressures to negotiate early, mandatory retirement ages for stewardesses continued.[23] In 1953, American Airlines advised its stewardesses that it would commence terminating them at thirty-two. By April 18, 1954, after discussing the issue with ALSSA, American was able to execute a memorandum of agreement that accomplished this goal and was retroactive to September 16, 1953.[24] The trend to ground stewardesses in their thirties had begun.

Other discriminatory patterns were developing among the carriers. More than a decade before the Equal Pay Amendment to the Fair

Labor Standards Act was passed in 1963, Victor Herbert advised Koos to negotiate equal salaries for stewards and stewardesses. In some cases airlines seemed willing to increase steward earnings over that of stewardesses, and Herbert held firm in his view of this as a negative trend. Koos elaborated that the minority male membership presented some "touchy" problems for ALSSA. Some of the women members considered the job a female domain and looked down on the male flight attendants.[25] Herbert lamented that some pilots also had difficulties with the idea of male flight attendants and did not like the idea of having a steward become president of an organization affiliated with ALPA.[26]

Before 1935, flight attendants throughout the world were almost exclusively male, but after World War II the American carriers hired females with only a few exceptions. Consequently, many pilots of the 1950s had never worked with male flight attendants. Some pilots and stewardesses considered the job too sissy a role for men. If a man or a woman ventured out of the more clearly defined heterosexual occupations he or she could be suspected of homosexuality. This societal attitude tainted what might have developed into better working relationships. In any case, the predominantly female jobs offered low pay compared to the male occupations. During most of the first forty years of the occupation, flight attendants' salaries were so low that it was difficult for a man to work the job and be the good provider that American society expected.

During her presidency, Koos married John Spencer, a Capital Airlines pilot. She knew that she would be unable to return to active status as a flight attendant after her leave was over. She planned to run for reelection, but by the time of the May 1953 convention, she was three months pregnant. Herbert encouraged her to remain a candidate despite her pregnancy. She did not publicize her pregnancy, and because only a few delegates knew of it, it was not an open issue at the convention.[27] Koos believed that ALPA encouraged her to run partially because of the possibility that a steward could win the presidency. The vice president, John Oliver, an Eastern flight attendant, wanted the job, and other stewards, particularly from Eastern Airlines, had been very active with the union.

At the 1953 convention a power struggle arose. Eastern's contingent, mostly married heads of households, was interested in preplotted, stable schedules, while Koos was advocating the industrywide goal of reducing monthly flying maximums to eighty-five hours. To draw off uncommitted support that might go to Koos in order to later bargain with her for a compromise position, Eastern ran Rowland K. Quinn, Jr., who held the highest elective union office at Eastern. Quinn remembered that after he arrived at the convention he was caught up in the politicking and suddenly emerged as the dark horse presidential candidate.[28] Surprisingly, he won.

To many ALSSA officers, there seemed to be an all-out effort on ALPA's part to thwart the flight attendants' efforts to achieve self-determination. Perhaps to fight fire with fire, the women chose a man to lead their organization. "Although the membership was almost all female," Edith Lauterbach explained, "many honestly believed, at that time, that a man would be more effective than a woman as president."[29]

Quinn was well equipped to handle the job. He had graduated from the University of Miami in 1950 with a degree in industrial management; he had minored in airline operation and economics. Hired as a steward by Eastern in 1950, Quinn became a local union officer for ALSSA in 1951. He was elected master executive council chairman in 1953. Pilots would have had difficulty questioning Quinn's manly image. Quinn had learned to fly airplanes the same year he graduated from high school and had spent two years with the U.S. Air Force stationed in Europe.[30]

Just before the 1953 convention, ALPA granted ALSSA a permanent charter of affiliation that gave ALSSA control of its own dues and limited power that would not be overridden by an ALPA liaison. Quinn wanted no part of working with an ALPA overseer and made that clear. Herbert said, "I was still the liaison with Quinn after he was elected, as far as ALPA was concerned. But Quinn did not want that, so I dropped into the background."[31] It was during that time that Herbert started working with the airline agents and other ground employees to guide them into the Air Line Employees Association, an autonomous union affiliated with ALPA.

While the convention directives of agency shop, acquisition of an independent charter through the A F of L, and certification still remained priorities, Quinn was quickly caught up in essential day-to-day business. When he took office, "there were twenty-eight airlines that I represented, and there were twenty-six open agreements that needed to be negotiated." The fifteen hundred members were paying $3.50 a month, and with less than half of the flight attendants supporting the union, "we were dying financially—no question about it."

Traveling from airline to airline, Quinn began negotiating on each property where ALSSA represented flight attendants. He quickly found that most carriers were adamantly against an agency shop provision for the stewardesses and stewards, "for the obvious reason that the organization would become stronger and possibly more militant."[32]

The ALSSA growth rate had been overwhelming; by 1953, it represented thirty-five hundred flight attendants. Now operating on a budget of its own, ALSSA had net cash reserves of $29,598 and total assets of $31,850; the union would need more money to offer essential and independent services.[33]

Quinn enjoyed a period of relative calm with the pilots' union from 1953 to 1957. He was easily reelected and began his second term by getting rid of any liaison between ALSSA and ALPA. While more workable, the relationship with the pilots' union was still undesirable to many: "I think that those of us in ALSSA, and I am speaking of the leadership, believed that we could get our own charter," Quinn said, "and we proceeded from time to time to ask AFL-CIO for a charter. A claim on the craft and class by virtue of its ability was recognized by the AFL-CIO, but they already had two federations representing flight attendants—ALPA and TWU." ALSSA wanted to sit in on the labor council because many of its actions during the 1950s directly affected flight attendants.[34]

Additional civil air regulations to cover flight attendants were attracting the interest of some legislators; in 1958 the Federal Aviation Act created the Federal Aviation Authority (FAA) to coordinate and to promote the safety of all aviation activities—private, commercial, and military. During the early 1950s ALSSA had sent a lobbyist, Iris Peterson, a UAL stewardess who had joined the union soon after its founding, to Washington, D.C. As a registered lobbyist, Peterson's strengths lay in being articulate and in the strict values of her Mormon upbringing in Idaho. Unflappable in her pursuit for improvements in her occupation, she presented testimony to Congress, filed lawsuits, and wrote safety regulations for various commercial aircraft.

While the ALSSA leadership on United supported in general the policies of Quinn's administration, some problems began to trouble the former ALSA women. Contractual agreements had not shown a marked improvement on the UAL property, and some members believed that in the quest for agency shop and union security provisions other items were being neglected. In the 1956–57 ALSSA agreement for UAL, an important item had been lost, differential pay whereby compensation for flight hours beyond sixty, sixty-five, or seventy was calculated according to the speed of the aircraft. The faster equipment had previously increased the earnings of United stewardesses. In the dawn of the jet age the UAL stewardesses had not yet come to realize how much they had lost in that single concession. Nothing substantial had been gained—such as union or agency shop—to offset this loss.

According to Paul Berthoud, company negotiator for UAL stewardess contracts from 1955 to 1962, when the differential pay according to speed was negotiated away by the union, no other carrier had pay tied to speed. The negotiations were leading to a flat monthly salary mainly because American Airlines used that method and at that time UAL stewardesses were not paid as well as American's. When the company negotiated with stewardesses, it was not unusual to deal with more issues than with other groups. In some cases whole sections of the contract were amended.[35]

The union leadership on United, which included some of Ada Brown's early officers and members, experienced some difficulty in dealing with the union leadership on Eastern and TWA. In Edith Lauterbach's opinion, the problems were with airline management as much as with the flight attendants. In the opinion of some, problems were brought on because Howard Hughes, the major shareholder in TWA, seemed only interested in a write-off: "TWA didn't seem genuinely concerned with stewardesses. By contrast, United wanted their stewardesses to be happy."[36]

By 1957 the question of ALSSA independence from ALPA intensified the friction. With renewed determination, the delegates to the 1957 convention made strong mandates to negotiate union shop agreements. With a budget of eighty thousand dollars and a projected budget of more than a hundred thousand dollars a year in the near future, the costs of representation for the growing membership were skyrocketing.[37] The delegates amended ALSSA's constitution to prevent ALPA from "seizing their organization." Further, they eliminated any provisions for an ALPA liaison officer. Reaction came quickly from the pilots. ALPA's executive committee notified Quinn that it did not ratify the amendments, which they considered in conflict with ALPA's rights.

Quinn replied to the pilots that "ALSSA is wholly owned and supported by the cabin attendants," and under that principle the board of directors for ALSSA had taken action to prevent the pilots from taking over their association. Any move of the pilots to initiate action to resume control over the stewardesses and stewards seemed to ALSSA inconsistent with the theory of an international charter. Quinn pointed out that in practice he had found the provisions pertaining to the liaison officer impossible and explained that for the past four years the ALPA liaison officer had existed on paper alone. For these reasons ALSSA had decided to eliminate the position.[38] The period of calm between pilots and flight attendants was over.

In 1958, several disputes centered around honoring picket lines. Facing the possibility of a strike, Eastern's ALSSA members sought guarantees from ALPA that the pilots would honor its picket lines. ALPA refused. Angered, Eastern's flight attendants signed a mutual assistance pact with Eastern's machinists union. No strike occurred, but the hostilities deepened. In late 1958, ALSSA struck Lake Central Airlines. ALPA crossed the ALSSA picket line and worked with scabs.

The 1959 ALSSA convention was heated by open charges, bitterness, and tension between ALSSA and ALPA. Quinn, now having served seven years as president of the flight attendant union, accused ALPA of paternalistic domination of the steward and stewardess union to further

ALPA's own ends and made it clear that the membership was not satisfied with ALSSA's situation. ALPA representatives at the convention contended the stewardesses' actions were illegal, ungrateful, and shortsighted. Quinn asked the ALPA representatives to give further consideration to ALSSA's quest for their own affiliation through AFL-CIO, independent of ALPA, and received their approval to look into the possibility. Realizing that they may have made a mistake, the representatives of ALPA then reneged by claiming that ALPA was empowered by their AFL-CIO charter to exercise a certain amount of direction over ALSSA. They threatened to oppose any attempt by the flight attendants to gain independence and promised to set up another association of stewardesses if ALSSA broke away. [39]

Underlying all the charges and countercharges between ALPA and ALSSA was a new and divisive technological development, the advent of the jet aircraft. The tenuousness of the relationship between ALPA and ALSSA was heightened by conflicting interests in planning for the future work lives of their members. The pilots had traditionally negotiated salaries on increments that could be tied to a base pay, mileage, night flying, weight, and capacity. Jet airplanes were fast and large, offering the pilots highly desirable working conditions. The so-called third seat in the cockpit was manned by the flight engineers, who were represented by the Flight Engineers International Association (FEIA), and now became a coveted position. The battle for jurisdiction over the third seat was bitter. [40] The pilot union's energies were being poured into blocking the flight engineers' claim to a workplace in the jet cockpit.

The increased speed of the jet and the added seating capacity often more than doubled the number of stewardesses' flights and intensified their passenger service duties. The women wanted relief in the form of reduction of hours on the jet. Although the pilots and flight attendants had totally separate contracts, conflicting demands regarding monthly maximum of hours to be flown could weaken either group's chances of achieving its goals.

Perhaps overanxious about losing jobs and still in the heated dispute with the engineers, the pilots wanted the flight attendants to abandon their goal of a reduction in hours. The ALSSA leadership believed that it was the time to pursue the item.

The breakthrough to achieve agency shop coincided with the delivery of jets to Trans World Airlines. The airline industry had balked at the agency shops. According to UAL negotiator Paul Berthoud, "At that time, the company had strong feelings against union shops." None had been negotiated by United in the 1950s, except with the International Association of Machinists and Aerospace Workers (IAM).[41]

The thaw for the agency shop came about accidentally. Quinn had helped negotiate a provision on Trans World Airlines that restricted flight hours within a given duty period to eight hours. There was an exception: flight attendants could fly up to ten hours on the 1049 G. Constellation. When TWA received their new Lockheed 1640 jet equipment, they arbitrarily applied the ten-hour exception to that equipment. Flight attendant resistance was spontaneous, and "there was a big work stoppage."[42]

TWA officials called on Quinn to end the wildcat strike. Quinn replied that he would end the work stoppage if TWA would agree to expedited arbitration. TWA agreed, but meanwhile, there was still the problem of flying shifts of more than eight hours on the new equipment. In order to continue long-segment routes that exceeded eight hours of flight time, TWA began new negotiations with ALSSA to reconsider the eight-hour restriction. Quinn drove a hard bargain: "I said that my price would be union [agency] shop, and TWA said that they would not be blackmailed. They then agreed to the agency shop."[43]

The jet age crew complement and reduction in hours became burning issues with flight attendants. ALSSA, under pressure to negotiate new working conditions, found that the burden fell mainly to TWA flight attendants because they now had the agency shop agreement and thus the resources to do the job. ALSSA became involved in a health study of jet equipment, a complicated effort that involved a ratio of speed, size, and flight attendant crew complement. Some women had complained about irregularities in their menstrual cycles, which they believed were brought on by the working conditions of the jet aircraft.

The study was rudimentary but nonetheless the first effort to review the effects of flying on stewardesses' health. The lowering of jet hours for flight attendants was tied to women's health and would become an emotional issue in collective bargaining.

Companies predictably belittled the idea that flight attendant health problems were connected with flying eighty-five hours a month in jet equipment. The pilots were going for maximum hours to achieve top earnings and were disinterested in health studies on jet travel. They would probably not support a strike over the issue of lowering of jet hours if that item caused ALSSA and TWA to come to deadlock on the contract. Quinn found himself in a political quandry.

Running behind in negotiating changes for work rules on the jets, ALSSA was bogged down in a three-way struggle: a continuing drive to obtain its own AFL-CIO federal charter, the pilot union's claim on their class and craft, and the growing interest of other unions, including the Teamsters and the Transport Workers Union, who also claimed the class and craft, in absorbing the flight attendants.

The United stewardesses and a few Hawaiian stewards came under particular stress. Under a contract that became amendable in 1959, the company applied conventional working conditions and rest periods maintained for propeller aircraft to the jet schedules. United's ALSSA membership was divided on the affiliation problems, and by the early 1960s, UAL would be involved in a merger with Capital Airlines that would make it the second largest airline in the world (surpassed only by the USSR's Aeroflot).

The union was in chaos when Rowland Quinn headed the ALSSA convention in Chicago during the first week of April 1959. Edith Lauterbach attended the convention in an unofficial capacity, and she acknowledged that many United members approved of Quinn's move to pull ALSSA out of the pilot union but were skeptical of alternative union affiliation possibilities.

Lauterbach recounted that the Teamsters had been invited to the 1959 convention and observed that the Teamsters initially showed interest in the stewards and stewardesses. They provided a representative from their union, but withdrew the guest speaker, Frank Fitzsimmons, an organizer for Teamster president Jimmy Hoffa, when the opposing groups grew more and more extreme in their views. Emotions ran high, and there was much back-door caucusing. Some delegates speculated that even the Teamsters came to the conclusion that the stewardesses were "too hot to handle."[44] It is just as likely that the Teamsters had evaluated the stewardesses as an unstable group that would be a poor risk for affiliation.

The claim was always made that the Teamsters were invited to the 1959 convention and that Quinn "was working on the outside—under the table, so to speak, in an arrangement with the Teamsters." But, although he later found out that a Teamster representative was in the hotel during the convention, he never met with the Teamsters.

It is true that the Teamsters were interested in the group, but "they stayed on the periphery and never made any real push for the stewards and stewardesses." Quinn made a statement that he "admired the strength of the Teamsters," but he recognized that the Teamsters "at that particular time, would never have been a salable item to the flight attendants."[45]

Amid the furor of the convention, ALPA pilot officials met with ALSSA's executive board April 3 and 4, 1959, and appointed an ALPA committee to work on the problems of the two organizations. For ALSSA's delegates, it was too little and too late, and on April 6, 1959, they voted to disaffiliate with ALPA. The fracture with the pilots' union had become irreconcilable, and Quinn pressed for an AFL-CIO independent charter, which the 1959 delegates had again mandated.

In response to ALSSA's request for a charter in November 1959, George Meany, president of AFL-CIO, informed Quinn that the AFL-CIO was respecting ALPA's rights to the group as defined by AFL-CIO's constitution (article III, section 7).[46] Under these provisions, the executive council of the AFL-CIO is restricted from issuing charters to affiliated unions except with the written consent of the parent union.

ALPA's claim, however, was not secure. ALPA had never appeared on a ballot on elections tallied by the National Mediation Board, and in all representational cases ALSSA had been the official bargaining agent. Moreover, ALPA's own constitution and bylaws restricted membership and officer candidacy of that union to only pilots. By maintaining their union by, for,and of pilots, ALPA had tried to have affiliates under control by appointed officers and liaisons. With the issuance of the 1953 permanent charter to ALSSA, the pilots had, in fact, created an autonomous union.

Although the argument of autonomy was strong, ALPA had given validity to the alliance between their union and the stewards and stewardesses by granting the conditional charter in 1947, the regular charter in 1951, and the permanent charter in 1953 to ALSSA. Quinn, himself, had recognized and used this benefit in 1957, when he had protested to the AFL-CIO regarding a Transport Workers Union raid on ALSSA's Northwest flight attendants.[47]

Immediately after his correspondence to Quinn, Meany wrote to Clarence Sayen, president of ALPA, with strong suggestions for how ALPA was to solve the stewardess problem: "As I pointed out to you during our last meeting in my office, your international union must assume the responsibility for the welfare and conduct of the Air Line Stewards and Stewardesses and I again urge you and recommend to you that immediate steps be taken by ALPA to establish within your international union, a Department or Division of Air Line Stewards and Stewardesses as a part of ALPA. This would bring about a closer relationship with your organization and the Air Line Stewards and Stewardesses."[48]

There were several reasons why the AFL-CIO wanted to patch up the strained and deteriorating relationship between ALSSA and ALPA. First, there were already two charters out to international unions that represented flight attendants. ALPA had been issued an A F of L charter in 1931, and the Transport Workers Union, a CIO union, represented flight attendants through the voluntary recognition extended by Pan American in 1946. TWU had opposed the AFL-CIO merger in 1955, and the further agitation of issuing a charter to flight attendants could give Michael Quill of the TWU new ammunition against the AFL-CIO.[49] Finally, and perhaps most important, it was now an appropriate time to pressure ALPA to change its restrictive constitution and bylaws to comply with the intent of the recently enacted Landrum-Griffin Act by changing the sections of its constitution and bylaws that would not meet the democratic test of the act.

After the 1959 convention a period of relative calm set in until July 15, 1960, when some ALSSA officers from United alleged election irregularities. ALPA, at the AFL-CIO's request, scheduled a hearing on the charges. Quinn did not attend the hearing, pointing out that ALPA had no authority over ALSSA pursuant to the dissolution resolution of the 1959 convention. The severely strained relationship between ALSSA and ALPA broke.

August 6, 1960, Quinn had the entire physical properties of the flight attendant offices in Chicago removed: desks, files, records, and even the carpeting were moved from the ALPA building at 55th and South Cicero Avenue to 316 West Randolph Street.

ALPA responded immediately. Its leaders instructed all ALSSA employees to report to work as if nothing had happened, held special meetings, revoked the permanent ALSSA charter, filed ten charges against Quinn, and appointed temporary officers as had been provided under the old conditional charter issued in 1947. [50]

The ALSSA rank and file was deeply split, and years of struggle for membership began. Officers and legal advisers from both sides went to work. ALPA went to court in August 1960, seeking restraining orders and permanent injunctions against the continuing functioning of ALSSA. In turn, Quinn and several supporters, including Janet Heisler and Helen Chase, original organizers for ALSSA, filed a claim seeking a judgment that they were the true and proper officials of ALSSA. The court denied ALPA's temporary injunction and ordered all parties to refrain from issuing misleading statements. [51]

The legal status of both ALSSA and ALPA as representatives of the flight attendants was unclear. The airlines, aware of the internal struggle of flight attendants with their union affiliation, deposited all checked off dues into escrow accounts in August 1960. [52] The cutoff of dues particularly hurt Quinn's faction. Ironically, it had been Quinn who had thrown support behind the checkoff provisions at negotiations, and in turn, it was mainly the flight attendants who had achieved union shop and checkoff on their airlines who supported Quinn. Now a large part of the income of ALSSA was cut off. The legal battles, which involved fifty-two suits and countersuits, further depleted ALSSA's resources. [53] In contrast, ALPA's assets in 1960 totaled around $4.5 million. [54]

While some local union work continued, Quinn reported to the AFL-CIO that airlines "have declined to continue negotiations with ALSSA or ALPA and to process grievances, including some cases of disciplinary discharge."[55]

At the United Airlines corporate headquarters negotiations for a stewardess contract were placed on an indefinite hold. Company negotiator Paul Berthoud explained that although the stewardesses' agreement was amendable, the company did not know with whom to negotiate, ALPA or ALSSA. During the Christmas holiday period in 1960, United made an unusual offer: the United stewardesses could obtain an interest-free loan. Berthoud said this idea was based on the company's knowledge that their stewardesses were being underpaid.[56]

It was clear that if ALPA was to become the bargaining representative for flight attendants it would have to secure the authorization-to-act cards under its name. The office left empty by Quinn at ALPA headquarters became an organizing center as United stewardesses came first to sign up members to be represented under ALPA.[57]

ALPA was under the leadership of a young, progressive Braniff pilot, Clarence Sayen, who had succeeded David L. Behncke to become ALPA's second president. The transfer of power had been difficult and costly to the union because the aging Behncke resisted retirement in the courts. A court-appointed receiver became suspect in the maintenance of ALPA funds, and before the pilots regained control of their union, it was nearly bankrupt.[58]

The airline industry had changed much during Behncke's guidance of ALPA. Although the constitution and bylaws of ALPA had been amended in the 1950s to make the union more democratic, when the dissident ALSSA split with ALPA, the pilot union could no longer afford the luxury of gradualist reforms. If it was to stay in the stewardess business, immediate changes to bring ALPA into compliance with the intent of the Landrum-Griffin Act were needed. Some pilots wanted the alternative of getting out of the stewardess business. They considered their union too important to be eroded by admittance of less professional workers.

The splintered rank-and-file flight attendants could be lost by ALPA, possibly to the newly formed International Guild of Flight Attendants that had the backing of Teamsters, unless an amended constitution could bring them into ALPA's fold, and Sayen needed an acceptable package to present to the ALPA board of directors at their meeting scheduled for November 1960. Proposals for an amended constitution and bylaws would have to meet the satisfaction of pilots, flight attendants, and the AFL-CIO, as well as comply with the Landrum-Griffin Act. ALPA set up an organizational structure study committee and called an emergency meeting on August 23, 1960. Nine stewardesses attended the meeting, and two, Sally Gibson of UAL and Fran Holmes of TWA, were elected to serve on the committee. The following day, Holmes and Gibson met with an organizational structure subcommittee to discuss the areas that were unacceptable to flight attendants (e.g., the initiation fees and penalties, and the lack of flight attendant representation on the ALPA executive committee).[59] Gibson also addressed the problem of union or agency shop. Although ALPA had remained opposed to agency or union shop, the pilots on the organizational structure study committee agreed that they might be willing to accept an agency shop for the flight attendant group, particularly a modified agency shop in which certain employees could be exempted from the requirement of paying union dues or becoming union members (i.e., those who were employed at the time the provision was negotiated). The modified agency shop concept would develop into a complicated effort to spare people with strong feelings against unionism any real or imagined indignity of having to become a member. On this issue the pilot union came close to sharing company management attitudes.

Clarence Sayen began dealing with the stewardess problem with the ALPA convention in Miami in November 1960. He had sent copies of proposals for affiliation agreements to the ALPA Board of Directors, and all other items on the agenda were overshadowed by the stewardess problem. Although Sayen himself was the really big issue within ALPA in the 1960–62 period, the internal politicking of ALPA focused dissension on the stewardess problem. Feelings of the delegates representing the 13,481 ALPA pilots ran high. In order to change their constitution and bylaws, a two-thirds majority vote was needed; one-third of the members were opposed to maintaining the stewardesses' affiliation with ALPA.

Early in the convention Sayen, who wanted to keep the flight attendant group as an affiliate of ALPA, managed to get a two-thirds vote to "stay in the stewardess business." With one-third of the delegates threatening a veto, Sayen used parliamentary procedures of the convention to stall until he could get a majority rule. The convention became a prolonged session of discussions regarding the advantages of trade unionism versus the drawbacks of industrial unionism. The divisions among delegates seemed unbridgeable, and moves to "get out of the stewardess business" were thwarted. At least one delegate thought he had initially voted to "explore all means of incorporating the stewardesses into ALPA or help them set up their own union," under a separate charter with no affiliation with ALPA.[60]

The delegates, both for and against the opening of the organization to other airline workers, felt threatened. Their arguments often overlapped, but the overriding theme of their statements was fear. The stewardess problem was almost entirely dealt with as a pilot problem. Certification, strikes, and tenure of over eighteen months for some stewardesses, especially union officers, were viewed as undesirable trends of this work group. One delegate noted that the "little girl" who became a stewardess got a taste of life at the same time that she looked for a husband, which was the real career for which she was brought up. "But this one little sneaker in this thing," he added, "[is that] the leaders of her organization stay." He berated the pilots, and himself, for not taking the flight engineers into their union when they had the opportunity.

Another opponent of bringing the stewardesses into a closer relationship claimed that "if the girls wanted to wear pink girdles and if the pilots didn't think they should, they could be in court all the time fighting over these things."[61]

The pilots were also concerned about being outnumbered by the stewardesses and had difficulties establishing numbers of flight attendants; calculations went from around eighty-five hundred up to about ten thousand five hundred. (In 1957 there were 9,450 flight attendants representing 6.4 percent of the airline work force, while 13,286 pilots represented 9.0 percent of the same work force.)[62] By the 1959 convention ALSSA was the collective bargaining representative for stewardesses on Alaska, Allegheny, Aloha, American, Bonanza, Braniff, Capital, Caribbean-Atlantic, Central, Continental, Eastern, Flying Tiger, Frontier, Great Lakes, Hawaiian, Lake Central, Mackey, National, North Central, Northeast, Northwest, Ozark, Pacific, Pacific Northern, Trans Texas, Trans World, United, West Coast, and Western. Almost all the flight attendants working on U.S. carriers were affiliated with ALSSA.

The stalling by parliamentary procedure caused the convention to drag on through the Thanksgiving holiday, and one delegate charged, ". . . this body is tired, fatigued, frustrated, nervous, exhausted, and we are tired of legal shenanigans and maneuverings." Whenever the affiliation question was discussed, the doors were closed to all but ALPA members; the stewardesses themselves were banned from discussions of their future. Finally on November 21, the organizational structure study committee submitted a second, revised, plan for convention approval. The ALPA proposals for restrictions on the election processes of officers if the stewardess and steward division was incorporated in ALPA were the most disputed items. A call was made to Representative Philip Landrum, a Georgia Democrat and one of the authors of the Landrum-Griffin Act. Landrum stated that he did not feel that the revised plan for restructuring the relationship of the two unions was in keeping with the intent of the law. Proposals were returned to committee for further study. The pilots were having difficulty accepting the intent of Landrum-Griffin because it meant that to represent the stewardesses they would have to change their association into a more democratic union.

On November 22, 1960, some of the pilots became very impatient, and Joseph DeCelles of TWA Council 3 made a resolution to offer that ALPA should help the stewards and stewardesses secure a separate charter. DeCelles claimed that a call had been made to AFL-CIO president George Meany and that Meany disclosed that he would issue a charter to the stewards and stewardesses if ALPA did not incorporate them into ALPA. Sayen ruled that such a resolution was out of order because the board had previously voted to take the stewards and stewardesses into ALPA.

Word began to circulate that George Meany had sent a telegram to Sayen stating that the AFL-CIO would grant the flight attendants a charter if ALPA did not take the steward and stewardess group into their organization. Asked by a delegate if this was true, Sayen explained that a telegram from Meany had reiterated the AFL-CIO position that "in the event the ALPA refused to open its Constitution and Bylaws to admit ALSSA as full members of ALPA, ALPA should then relinquish their right to represent ALSSA and allow the AFL-CIO to issue a dual charter to the ALSSA." Sayen pointed out that Meany was somewhat confused on this issue; ALPA had already made the decision to accommodate flight attendants, and, in any case, it was a local federal charter that AFL-CIO would grant to ALSSA, not an international charter. [63]

The convention was almost worn down, and although a vote to pass the resolution for a steward and stewardess division had failed to pass on three previous roll call votes, passage now seemed imminent. The amendment was again put to voice vote before the remaining delegates. Although it was later pointed out that under ALPA's constitution and bylaws a roll call vote is required where a fixed majority is necessary, the voice vote was declared to have carried. [64]

The membership problem was temporarily and partially solved. As a result of the pilots' 1960 convention, the ALPA organizational structure was changed radically. Unlike any other union in the United States it embodied two discrete organizations, the Pilot Division and the Stewards and Stewardesses Division (S & S Division). Each group would adopt its own constitution and bylaws, and henceforth ALPA would be governed by two documents. Now ALPA could launch an organizational blitz to affiliate ALSSA members.

The next month ALSSA came close to obtaining its own charter or, at the least, was irresponsibly led into believing so by officials of the AFL-CIO. Quinn, told the ALSSA delegates in 1961, "At one point, in my search for the Holy Grail, the AFL-CIO told me that Mr. Meany had authorized the issuance of a charter to ALSSA. . . ."[65] In December 1960, ALSSA officers were summoned to Washington, D.C., to receive a charter. B. J. Stewart, a United flight attendant, confirmed the meeting with AFL-CIO officials to receive a charter. According to her, AFL-CIO officials posed for photographs with the ALSSA contingency, holding up a paper that resembled a charter. The ALSSA group was told that the details of the charter would be drawn up later and that by the time the ALSSA representatives returned to Chicago the charter

74

would be waiting for them. But, Stewart said, "I never saw the photographs of that meeting."[66]

The AFL-CIO, with only a minority of female workers, had never chartered a union led and dominated by women at all levels. This was partially because the AFL-CIO had consistently been more comfortable with male leadership of all unions, including predominantly female unions; but also the unions formed by stewardesses are the only such groups that the AFL-CIO could have chartered. In 1960 the idea of chartering a union of short-term female workers must have frightened the AFL-CIO officers.

Seven months after the organizational restructuring of ALPA, the AFL-CIO executive council called a meeting of the ALPA leadership, ALPA-ALSSA supporters, and Rowland Quinn, president of ALSSA, along with dissident officers from ALSSA. Meany addressed the parties, saying, "We are not here to settle problems, but to determine the problems as seen by AFL-CIO." Sensitive to the provisions of the new Landrum-Griffin Act, Meany listened to changes in ALPA's structure as presented by ALPA president Clarence Sayen, and it quickly became apparent that the AFL-CIO was supportive of Sayen's efforts to retain the representational rights for the flight attendants. Put on the defensive, the Quinn representation was asked to justify certain actions taken by ALSSA.[67]

To the AFL-CIO it may have appeared that ALSSA could be brought back into the fold of ALPA by the reforms and good faith on the part of the pilot union. But this underestimated two problems: Quinn's dissidents would not be placated by an amended and somewhat questionable constitution, and the Transport Workers Union was willing to risk expulsion by the AFL-CIO in its quest for representational rights for dissident flight attendants.

With its mounting expenses, ALSSA would have to find affiliation somewhere. If it tried to remain independent, it would be vulnerable to raiding from ALPA and others. Affiliation possibilities were extremely limited because of the AFL-CIO's no-raid pact. Quinn, with other ALSSA officers, met with TWU officials, each group accompanied by attorneys, on January 20, 1961, and by March 1961, ALSSA made application by letter to TWU for a charter of affiliation. Michael J.

Quill, president of TWU responded by March 6, 1961, advising that the TWU executive council had voted to grant a charter to ALSSA.[68] The application for the charter and affiliation with the TWU by ALSSA was in defiance of an order from George Meany, who was unable to dissuade the TWU from what he considered a raid on another AFL-CIO union, thus putting the TWU in conflict with AFL-CIO policies and rules.[69] ALSSA, ALPA, TWU, and AFL-CIO leaders fell into a legal quagmire. New litigation commenced simultaneously with the race for flight attendant representation.

During 1961, ALPA filed petitions with the National Mediation Board to represent flight attendants on twenty-one airlines, for which groups ALSSA was the certified bargaining representative. Quinn requested that the NMB grant ALSSA a hearing to provide the opportunity to prove that ALPA pilots were supervisors of the stewardesses and hence could not properly represent stewardesses for purposes of collective bargaining. The request was denied. At the same time, ALSSA filed suit in U.S. district court for the District of Columbia to enjoin elections until hearings were held by the NMB. The court held that it did not have jurisdiction to compel the NMB to conduct a hearing.[70]

Rowland Quinn's prediction to ALPA that "if ALSSA and ALPA ever did fracture, the membership would be split about fifty-fifty," was being fulfilled. Quinn believed that UAL and the small carriers would stay with the pilots' union and the larger regional carriers that had achieved agency shop and had opted for self-determination would go with the group that had severed its affiliation.[71] Small carriers, such as Frontier and Hawaiian Airlines, worked in a more paternalistic company environment and usually had small airplanes with one stewardess working as a dependent crew member with the pilots. United members were somewhat different from those on other large airlines in that they seemed to maintain comfortable and happy relations with the pilots.

Quinn was correct. During 1961 and 1962, there were twenty-nine elections between TWU and ALPA for bargaining rights on properties where ALSSA had prior rights. These involved 8,700 flight attendants. ALPA's S & S Division won twenty elections, which accounted for approximately 3,580 flight attendants. Official ballot counts by the National Mediation Board showed that the representation for ALSSA and ALPA was about evenly split. The large regional carriers, including American, Eastern, Northeast, Northwest, Trans World, and Western Airlines had opted for the Transport Workers Union; they were soon joined by flight attendants on Trans-Texas and Caribbean-Atlantic. These former ALSSA members, representing the organization severed from ALPA, became Local 550 of the Transport Workers Union.

The irreconcilable schism in ALSSA affected four out of every five flight attendants; of the attendants on major carriers, only those on Delta, who remained without a union, and those on Pan Am, who had been represented by TWU since 1946, did not cast votes. At final tally, the S & S Division comprised attendants on United Airlines—the largest of all U.S. carriers—and nineteen other airlines, including Alaska, Allegheny, Aloha, Braniff (the first to join S & S Division on March 13, 1961), Capital, Continental, Frontier, Hawaiian, Mohawk, National, North Central, Overseas National, Ozark, Pacific Northern, Piedmont, Slick, and West Coast Airlines. These were joined by Airlift International in March 1962 and New York Airways in June 1963. Shortly thereafter, Western Airlines stewardesses voted to leave TWU, and they returned to ALPA in May 1964.[72]

The basic structure of the unions for stewardesses and stewards was determined for the next decade. The militant women had been held at bay because, as Rowland Quinn put it, "they just did not have the vehicle that they would later have through the women's movement." He believed that the women he worked with throughout the 1950s were just as militant as the structure of the organization would tolerate and likened their situation to "not being able to dive off the high board daily and survive very long."[73]

TWU quickly reneged on its affiliation promises with ALSSA. On January 15, 1962, TWU instructed Quinn to notify all the airlines that had dues checkoff agreements to send the monies directly to the TWU headquarters. Because there was no provision in the TWU constitution and bylaws that required checked off dues to be paid to the TWU, ALSSA's management committee unanimously voted to refuse. On March 3, 1963, Quill again notified Quinn, this time in writing, to have direct remittance of checkoff dues to the TWU, saying TWU would withdraw ALSSA's charter if they did not comply. ALSSA refused, and TWU did not withdraw the charter.[74] The amount of dues that airlines held in escrow for the ALSSA flight attendants was more than one hundred thousand dollars by July 1963.[75] Legal fees had mounted for ALSSA during the four-year turmoil, and on April 25, 1963, TWU directed Quinn to terminate his retainer agreement with the law firm of Leibik and Weyand. Although TWU had given ALSSA autonomous control over employment of legal counsel, Quinn complied.

Two months after Quinn was elected for a sixth term as president of ALSSA at the April 1963 biennial convention, the TWU, without notice, charges, or a hearing, imposed a trusteeship on ALSSA. TWU considered the charter and constitution and bylaws of ALSSA suspended and refused to permit any officer or committee of ALSSA to function without the consent of the trustee. Quinn, Helen Chase, and Janet Heisler were suspended from their offices of president, secretary, and treasurer.[76]

In unspecific charges, Quinn was accused of failing to carry out his obligation as president of ALSSA under its constitution and bylaws. Denied counsel, he was tried by the TWU international executive council on July 30, 1963, in New York City. A United States district court later determined that the hearing was not impartial in that a majority of the council had participated in the events involved in the charges. The court noted that Quill "berated Rowland K. Quinn, Jr. with vilification as a cheap-skate and disloyal union member. . . ." The court concluded that "the true and sole reason for the action of TWU in imposing the trusteeship and removing the plaintiff Quinn from office as President of ALSSA was to gain control of the income of ALSSA."[77]

The court restored Quinn to office. TWU appealed the case, and the appeals court reversed the order of the lower court on the grounds that the court lacked jurisdiction because the Landrum-Griffin Act applied only to members, not to leaders, of unions. One and a half years out of work, more than seventeen thousand dollars in personal debt for legal fees, and discredited among the membership by the charges, Quinn could not afford to retry the case. He went to work for the National

Mediation Board, where he now serves as the highly respected executive secretary.

The fifty-two suits and countersuits involving ALPA and ALSSA were settled in May 1963. ALPA waived any objection to the use of the name of ALSSA by Quinn's group, and nineteen thousand dollars in withheld dues was restored to ALPA and eighty-three thousand dollars to ALSSA. ALPA released the bank accounts it had frozen in 1960, and both parties withdrew claims to property, including files.[78]

While Quinn had been combating the affiliation problems for ALSSA with the Transport Workers Union, the flight attendants in the S & S Division of ALPA began trying to become a viable unit within the pilot union. The most glaring conflict with the Landrum-Griffin Act lay in the restrictions for members of the S & S Division on seeking candidacy for certain ALPA offices, specifically the presidency of ALPA. This issue had surfaced in an investigative meeting with the AFL-CIO, and George Meany addressed this inequity, saying that under the Landrum-Griffin Act there are no such things as second-class membership or limitations on seeking office. Sayen had answered Meany's concern by saying that he would not presume to interpret the Landrum-Griffin Act and that interpretation of the act would take much legal action.[79]

Aside from the election of the national officers of ALPA, the newly formed S & S Division had much in common with the predecessor unions of ALSSA and Ada Brown's independent ALSA. Both earlier unions had been patterned after ALPA, and many of the original ideas had survived. Under the S & S Division's separate-but-equal status, the members elected the local council chairman (later called chairperson) directly at each domicile. These chairmen formed the master executive council, which elected executive council officers, including the chairman (MECC). The job of the MECC included, but was not limited to, representing the union to a higher level of airline management. The local council chairmen formed the board of directors, the highest governing body of the S & S Division. The board of directors could and did write policy through its own constitution and bylaws. As members of the board of directors, the local officers could cast votes for some of ALPA's national officers.

The flight attendant groups at all airlines represented by the S & S Division retained autonomy on that carrier's property. Negotiations on each property remained separate and in the control of the negotiators appointed or elected by each master executive council. At the national level the highest ranking officer for the flight attendants was elected only by the S & S Division. Although the office was designated vice president, Stewards and Stewardesses Division, the office power was equivalent to chief executive of the S & S Division.

In November 1960, the active membership of ALPA was 13,481 pilots; after the representational elections, ALPA's membership increased by the 3,580 flight attendants in the S & S Division.[80] The number of flight attendants ALPA was required to represent came close to 5,000, and few union security provisions had been negotiated to support the carrying out of this obligation. Even by the most conservative estimates, it was, monetarily, a losing proposition for ALPA to represent steward and stewardesses.

The unequal partnership of the ALPA pilots and stewardesses in the early 1960s seemed natural to many. The airline industry's acceptance and implementation of discriminatory policies for stewardesses, such as the no-marriage rule, were well established. With such an unstable work force, the pilots had no need to fear the stewardesses even threatening to cast block votes to elect the president of ALPA.

4
The Unions and Women's Issues

The founders of the first stewardess union had formed the association in part to help bring about change in the traditionally accepted ideas of woman's place. The group worked mainly for higher salaries, better working conditions, and increased job security. But for the next three decades they and their successors continued to come up against the bastions of male supremacy.

"Use them till their smiles wear out; then get a new bunch," was the policy that had been put into effect by the airlines.[1] Their practices discriminated against stewardesses on the bases of sex, marital status, and age. In addition, airlines often formed unofficial company policies to deal with the "fat" stewardess and the unwed pregnant stewardess, and the stewardess's dress was governed by a wide array of regulations pertaining to everything from girdles to be worn under pencil slim skirts to high-heeled shoes. The job was open mainly to Caucasian women, although a few racially mixed, Oriental, native American, and Hispanic women were hired as stewardesses. Any hiring of minority women was an exception rather than part of an overall plan by the airline officials. Several airlines, including United and Capital Airlines, which merged with United in the early 1960s, experimented sparingly with hiring black women as stewardesses before the passage of the Civil Rights Act of 1964.

Preconditioned to think of themselves as short-term workers and harassed by a multitude of appearance and behavior requirements, stewardesses often did leave for the more socially acceptable role of wife and mother. "If you wanted to make points with a stewardess," pilot Jack O'Neill recalled of conditions in the 1950s and 1960s, "you didn't take her to dinner, you bought groceries and took them to her apartment so all her roommates could eat. Poor kids, they had a fast turnover, usually lasting six months to a year, and received a low salary, out of which company deductions for uniforms were made. If they didn't meet somebody better they went back home and married the local guy."[2]

Kelly Rueck, an active and high-ranking union officer during the late 1960s and early 1970s asserted, "Management's treatment of us as small children who couldn't possibly do anything right or think for ourselves discouraged many of us from continuing with the job or from taking an interest in seeing that the job itself was improved. . . . We were a fragmented, non-union-oriented, and disorganized collection of individuals, each with her own ideas about what should be done and how to do it."[3]

The advertising, hiring, and training policies of United throughout the 1960s made it apparent that the job was considered an interlude before the stewardess fulfilled the traditional woman's role of wife and mother. Discriminatory practices were so traditional and pervasive for stewardesses that they were often regarded as normal and natural. By 1961 United was receiving an average of fifty thousand applications a year for the job of stewardess. For each one accepted, one hundred fifty were rejected.[4] By 1965, the U.S. airlines collectively were interviewing around one million young women to fill only around ten thousand stewardess positions. American Airlines, in 1965, reported that 80 percent of its hostesses resigned because of marriage.[5]

It was difficult for women to break into the managerial ranks and even more unusual for them to be promoted within the hierarchy.[6] The one notable exception among most U.S. carriers was lower managerial levels in the stewardess or hostess service, where women were a majority. But ironically, in the dawn of the self-examining decade of the 1960s, United Airlines reversed its traditional policy of female management for stewardess offices. In the late 1950s UAL had appointed a committee of low- and middle-level management to appraise the stewardess job. After touring the system, the management team came to the conclusion that stewardesses were immature, irresponsible, and in need of constant supervision. That report stung the United stewardess union leaders. Their members possessed a high level of education and were expected to assume the stewardess job with professionalism, initiative, and loyalty.[7]

As a consequence of the report, United changed to visible and direct male supervision at stewardess domiciles. Demoted chief stewardesses could become staff assistants to the male managers or take other lower level positions. With few exceptions, chief stewardesses had difficulty accepting the new structure. Some Denver-based stewardesses watched as their chief stewardess, Jean Tippi, relinquished her office and was moved into a small, windowless cubicle. Tippi returned to active status as a rank-and-file stewardess, as did most other chief stewardesses. Sally Watt, the Seattle chief stewardess, who had more than fifteen years of managerial experience, was considered for the new position, but she lost out to a married male, who had a family to support and had recently been declared surplus by his previous department.[8] The level of management stewardesses encountered was often considered petty; more severe evaluations charged incompetence.

Of all the discriminating traditional requirements, that of single marital status had the most pronounced and long-term effect on the stewardesses individually and collectively. The constant turnover had an unsettling effect on union solidity and prevented the cohesiveness vital in demanding equitable compensation for services. The result was that few—the airlines, the unions holding bargaining rights, and often the stewardesses themselves—took the stewardesses seriously.

The average career for a stewardess on UAL remained short, and the turnover seemed highly desirable to United management. A UAL senior vice president commented in 1965, "If it got up to thirty-five months, I'd know we were getting the wrong kind of girl. She's not getting married."[9] Negotiating with stewardesses who were employed on a long-term basis would mean contracts that included provisions for retirement, health insurance, and other costly items; and some managers may have been able to perceive that a union of highly educated and skilled married women, who had the advantage of a second income, could survive a long strike. Also, many stewardesses could rely on alternate employment using traditional female skills (e.g., nursing or secretarial skills). A group of married stewardesses could represent an unusually powerful force compared to other unions whose members were predominantly male breadwinners.

Attacking the industry's no-marriage rules through collective bargaining seemed hopeless, especially since many stewardesses themselves often supported the companies' no-marriage policies. During the 1940s and 1950s, however, limited attempts were made to change the marital restrictions for stewardesses. Rowland Quinn negotiated for flight attendants on Aloha and Hawaiian Airlines in the 1950s. The Hawaiian women wanted to be married and continue their flying jobs. The inter-island hops made by the Hawaiian airlines were short, and the flight crews were able to be home every night. But the management negotiator's response to marriage for stewardesses was, "'We will negotiate for them to be pregnant but not married.'" Quinn asked, "Aren't you getting the cart before the horse?"[10]

Unions representing stewardesses also tried to use their grievance procedures to attack the no-marriage rule. As early as 1948, the Pan American marital policy was attacked by the Transport Workers Union (TWU). The union lost at the System Board of Adjustment when the arbitrator supported the company's right to continue its practices and policies as long as there was no contractual commitment against it.[11] In 1952 ALSSA represented a Trans World flight attendant and in 1959 a member employed by Eastern Airlines in cases involving marriage rules. Both were denied.

The referee's decision in the 1948 Pan American case included, ". . . that the function of the System Board is to interpret and apply the agreement in order to decide disputes that are properly before it, and that the Board has neither the duty nor the competence to resolve issues of public policy."[12] In general, arbitrators' decisions adhere to the realm of the collective bargaining agreement. While they are often asked to determine "proper cause" for discharge, most referees rule, as much as possible, within the parameters of the contractual agreement. Some argue that arbitrators cannot apply external laws. Another body of opinion claims that arbitrators can apply external laws and have done so in the application of state protective laws.[13] During the 1950s, however, the arbitrators making determinations on the airlines' discriminatory policies and practices had few, if any, external laws to consider.

A way to attack the no-marriage rule for stewardesses came in the form of Title VII, part of the Civil Rights Act of 1964, which became effective in 1965. Women were slow to use this new tool to gain their legal rights in the employment relationships, but the courts were even slower to accept sex as a basis of discrimination.

The sex discrimination provisions were added to the act in an amendment proposed by Representative Howard Smith, chairman of the House Ways and Means Committee. He was an outspoken opponent of the act, and his intent was apparently to prevent passage of the act by adding an unpopular section. He and other supporters of the sex discrimination amendment, including Representatives Dowdy and Pool of Texas, Tuten of Georgia, Andrews and Huddleston of Alabama, Rivers and Watson of South Carolina, and Gathings of Arkansas voted against the bill as finally drafted.[14]

Under the act, the Equal Employment Opportunity Commission (EEOC) issues employment guidelines and letters of opinion on whether a given practice violates the act. But while the commission is empowered to hear complaints and to issue opinions in cases where sex discrimination is charged, it does not exercise judicial power. The courts are free to agree or disagree with EEOC guidelines, but in practice, these are accorded substantial weight.

The Citizens Advisory Council on the Status of Women recommended to the EEOC adoption of certain policies, primary among which was that the bona fide occupational qualification (BFOQ) be interpreted narrowly. The council reported that very few jobs cannot be effectively performed by persons of either sex.[15]

The courts were slow to recognize that sex discrimination played a key role in the marriage policy. The first case to raise the issue was filed in 1967 by Eulalie E. Cooper, a stewardess with Delta Airlines. Cooper was fired on April 1, 1966, because the company officials learned she had married on October 17, 1964. In *Cooper v. Delta Airlines, Inc.*, the court looked only at the category of stewardess, saw that only women were included, and decided that the discrimination was not between men and women but rather between married women and single women.

Cooper's trial judge remarked that "the addition of sex to the prohibition against discrimination based on race, religion or national origin just sort of found its way into the equal employment opportunities section of the Civil Rights Bill. . . ."[16]

The judge was correct about the intent of its origins, but his decision in *Cooper* was without the benefits of the EEOC opinions. At the time *Cooper* was decided, the EEOC had not taken a position on whether discrimination based on marital status constituted sex-based discrimination if applied only to one sex. The case law regarding the no-marriage rule was off to an unfortunate start.

Prompted by complaints from ex-stewardesses who had been terminated due to marriage and requests from airlines for a general statement, the EEOC conducted a long study of sex discrimination in the airline industry. On June 20, 1968, the agency issued two opinions holding that the marital restrictions for stewardesses violated Title VII. The first was *Neal* v. *American Airlines, Inc.*, in which the termination of a stewardess six months after her marriage was contractually negotiated. The agreement provided the company an option to release from employment a married stewardess at any time six months after her marriage. The Air Transport Association argued this restriction avoided the danger of having pregnant stewardesses fly. The commission held that the provision discriminated on the basis of sex within the meaning of Title VII and rejected the company claim that, since all holders of the position of flight attendants on American were women, there could be no discrimination based on sex.

The second case in which the EEOC found the no-marriage policy in violation of the law was *Colvin* v. *Piedmont Aviation, Inc.*, in which the facts paralleled *Neal* except that the airline employed both male and female flight attendants. The marital restrictions did not apply to the stewards, many of whom married while employed. Although the EEOC consistently reaffirmed its holdings in *Neal* and *Colvin*, unfortunately, the commission's position was not immediately taken up by the courts.[17]

Most of the airlines bargaining with the S & S Division of ALPA began relaxing the no-marriage rule before the EEOC guidelines became solidified. There was one notable and potentially harmful exception, United Airlines. As the largest U.S. carrier, United persistently held to its rule, replacing and adding stewardesses at an unprecedented rate. From 1965 through 1970, UAL hired 10,295 stewardesses compared to the previous nine-year period, 1955 to 1964, when it had replaced and added a total of 7,488 stewardesses.[18] UAL was experiencing unusual growth during the late 1960s, due in part to the impending delivery of the jumbo jets; and the prevailing attitude was "'the flight attendants are ours,' and the very thought of changing the rules was reprehensible. It was like heresy."[19]

Clearly the union leadership and the social times were ahead of management requirements for stewardesses in the 1960s. In fact, the Stewards and Stewardesses Division of ALPA attempted to negotiate away the no-marriage rule before the enactment of the Civil Rights Act of 1964. The union's August 20, 1963, opening proposal clearly expresses the intention of abolishing United's policy of terminating flight attendants upon their marriage. In the negotiations for the 1965–66 agreement, United rejected any change in its no-marriage rule: "Stewardesses should discontinue flying upon marriage and raise families."

Rachel Woodings, chairwoman for the S & S Division committee, reported that when the S & S Division negotiations committee entered the 1967–69 negotiations, "the union team was aware of the prohibitions of the Civil Rights Act against sex discrimination and sought, consistent with the act, to abolish United's no-marriage policy." This time the union team tried to enter into the contract a proposal reading, "There shall be no discrimination whatsoever against and/or between employees covered by this Agreement because of age, sex, creed, color, or national origin."[20] The previous agreement of 1965–66 had included an antidiscrimination provision that covered race, creed, color, or national origin, and the union team had inserted only the word sex into the new proposal. United would not consider adopting this proposal. In the S & S Division's request for mediation, one of the important issues discussed with the aid of a representative of the National

Mediation Board was UAL's stonewalling of the no-marriage issue for stewardesses. But the union was not successful in abolishing the marriage prohibition.

Coinciding with the negotiations for the 1967–69 agreement was an important no-marriage case before the System Board of Adjustment at United. Terry Baker Van Horn had married in 1963 and did not disclose her marriage to the company. When the company found out in 1966 that Van Horn was married, she was fired. Van Horn filed a charge of discrimination with the EEOC on January 25, 1966, but a year later when the arbitration board was reviewing her case, no decision had been issued by the EEOC. Some union representatives were hopeful that the system board's decision on Van Horn would prompt a relaxing of the no-marriage rule at United. In an earlier arbitration, Braniff Airlines flight attendants, also represented by ALPA's S & S Division, had been upheld in a no-marriage case on September 14, 1965; but in a subsequent decision, an arbitrator refereeing an American Airlines no-marriage case wrote, "It is best to state bluntly and with all candor that I do not regard the Braniff case as a persuasive precedent to guide this Board."

On April 21, 1967, the arbitrator ruling on the Van Horn case held that the arbitration board did not have jurisdiction to evaluate the no-marriage policy or to interpret Title VII; the grievant knew of the policy when she was hired; and the union had been unsuccessful in negotiating away the no-marriage policy, which antedated the first collective bargaining agreement between United and the union.[21] Woodings believed that "this decision, in the midst of negotiations, undoubtedly strengthened the resolve of United to resist any efforts by the union to abolish the no-marriage policy, or to include any prohibition against discrimination by reason of sex."[22]

During 1967, the EEOC questioned forty-eight airlines regarding marital restrictions. Of the twenty-five that responded, twelve did not impose any marital restriction, two had options, not recently exercised, to terminate stewardesses after six months of marriage, six terminated stewardesses upon marriage, and five had varying policies.[23] In June 1968 the EEOC's opinions holding that the marital restrictions for stewardesses violated Title VII were released.

At that time, ALPA's S & S Division held the bargaining rights for twenty-five of the nation's carriers, United being the largest. Of these, only United, Frontier, and New York Airways did not permit stewardesses to marry. [24] In November 1968, United, apparently in response to mounting pressure to allow flight attendants to continue in their positions after marriage, requested that ALPA send representatives to meet with United to discuss the no-marriage policy. [25]

United was the last of the major trunk carriers to eliminate the no-marriage rule. Company negotiators moved very cautiously. At first, the company was willing only to eliminate its nearly forty-year-old policy, but at ALPA's insistence also agreed to provide an opportunity for reinstatement of those individuals who had filed either a grievance or charges with the EEOC with respect to United's policy. The S & S Division sought back pay for flight attendants who were to be reinstated, but United proposed a provision that all back pay claims be dropped as a condition of reinstatement, which the union refused. No provision for back pay was made. The company, however, did agree that it would not take any action against stewardesses who had married in secret and were still flying.

The implementation of these new contract provisions did not go smoothly. United refused to reinstate individuals who were eligible for reinstatement under the agreement but were insisting on their rights to back pay. The union team believed the company was attempting to negotiate with some ex-stewardesses on an individual basis. In meetings held with the company in January 1969, it was agreed that individuals otherwise eligible to return would not be turned down if they refused to drop back pay claims.

In the 1969 negotiations, United spent much effort trying to keep to a minimum the reinstatement of stewardesses terminated because of the no-marriage rule and to block back pay provisions. The company proposal for reinstatement was confined to "management people"—stewardess supervisors, stewardess instructors, and stewardess appearance counselors. Even within that modest proposal there were company restrictions. It had selected March 1, 1965, as the cutoff date of hire, because that was the earliest time the stewardess supervisors were allowed to marry and continue their jobs. Also, UAL's negotiators stated that they could withstand any attack under the Civil Rights Act since the effective date of the act was July 2, 1965.

No agreement was reached on the wording of the provisions concerning reinstatement of former stewardesses until October 16, 1969, and then the agreement fell short of the union's position. It provided that the company would offer to any stewardess currently employed whose tenure had been continuous and to any manager or specialist the opportunity to return to active service with no loss of seniority, subject to the need for additional stewardesses after January 1, 1970. But the issue was far from being settled, and in early 1970, discussions were held on the issue of back pay for the former stewardesses who had been reinstated. The company refused to reach any agreement on the back pay issue. [26]

A review of the financial health of United Airlines during the period when the no-marriage and reinstatement issues were discussed shows that the liabilities for back pay for stewardesses would have been manageable for United Airlines. Stewardess pay was modest, and within the social climate of the times some women would have, undoubtedly, opted to stay in their homemaking roles. In 1967, UAL enjoyed net earnings of $76.19 million, up from $39.12 million in 1966. [27] Furthermore, during this period there were numerous openings for stewardesses at United. It hired 2,140 stewardesses in 1968, 1,745 in 1969, and 1,471 in 1970. [28] The maximum back pay, at the time of the initial no-marriage negotiations, that any stewardess would have been entitled to receive under Title VII would have been amounts for around three years. Effective on October 1, 1967, the starting pay for United stewardesses was $345 base pay with increments up to ten years. One in the fifth year of flying earned $445 monthly and one in the tenth year earned a monthly maximum base salary of $520. [29]

The issues of reinstatement and back pay would have to be thrashed out in the courts. Litigation from Title VII cases continued, with some companies taking the legal position that unions could be liable for the effects of sex discrimination, for example, wage differentials.

Legal advisers to ALPA were aware of possible implications to unions from sex-based discrimination. As early as 1970 a legal director cautioned that "unions as well as employers must refrain from sex discrimination in employment."[30] The issue was addressed by the Supreme

Court in *Northwest Airlines* v. *Transport Workers Union, AFL-CIO, et al.* on April 20, 1981. Mary Laffey, a female cabin attendant employed by Northwest, commenced a class action suit against Northwest in 1970. She challenged the legality of the wage differential between pursers and stewardesses. The job of purser was open only to males. Laffey won the Title VII case. Back pay, damages, and interest to the members of the Laffey plaintiff class amounted to more than $20 million. Northwest subsequently filed suit, charging that under the Equal Pay Act of 1963 and Title VII the union was partly responsible because the company and union had collectively bargained the conditions found to be unlawful; thus, the union should share the damages. The Supreme Court ruled that Northwest had neither a federal statutory nor a federal common law right to contribution from the union.[31]

The S & S Division of ALPA remained closely involved in most litigation of the no-marriage remedies. Sponsored by the union, *Sprogis* v. *United Airlines*, a Title VII suit, was filed in the U.S. District Court in Chicago. The district court, and, on appeal, the U.S. Court of Appeals for the Seventh Circuit held that United's no-marriage policy violated Title VII. Sprogis was reinstated.[32] In a second suit, *Romasanta* v. *United Airlines*, the U.S. district court denied certification of class action for flight attendants who were discharged or resigned and who had protested their resignation. The seventh circuit court refused to hear an appeal on the class issues,and the individual cases of the flight attendants in *Romasanta* were tried and decided or settled.[33] The union decided not to sponsor further litigation by plaintiffs in the case.

The *Romasanta* case was reactivated when Liane McDonald, who had been discharged in September 1968 but had not filed a protest by EEOC charge or grievance, moved to intervene in October 1975 in the *Romasanta* case and to process an appeal to obtain a class action. United resisted, and the district court denied her intervention as untimely. On appeal by McDonald, the seventh circuit, in 1976, reversed the district court, holding that her intervention was timely and that she could pursue a class action. United appealed, and in 1977, the U.S. Supreme Court, in a five-to-three decision, affirmed that McDonald had a right to intervene in the case.[34]

On return of the case to the U.S. District Court in Chicago in 1978, the court found that the class should be flight attendants who were discharged because of marriage between 1965 and November 1968. McDonald appealed, seeking a broader class, and the seventh circuit reversed the district court by holding that the class should include those who were discharged or resigned involuntarily because of the no-marriage rule between late October 1965 and November 1968. United petitioned, but in June 1979, the Supreme Court refused to hear a petition by UAL. This did not mean that the Supreme Court affirmed the seventh circuit decision, but only that the Supreme Court decided not to review the decision. The district court would for the first time be turning its attention to questions of individuals to be legitimately included in the class and remedies for class members.[35]

The *McDonald* case had reached a critical point for the union representing the active flight attendants, by now no longer the S & S Division but its successor the Association of Flight Attendants (AFA). The system seniority list of July 1, 1979, showed that approximately 6,055 of United's 9,123 flight attendants were hired after November 7, 1968, when the no-marriage rule was abolished. If all the *McDonald* women were reinstated with full seniority rights, about two-thirds of United's first long-term flight attendant work force could be affected by loss of relative seniority, diluted bidding rights, and furloughs. In addition, the remaining 3,068 flight attendants hired before November 1968 could be affected, depending on the overlapping seniority of the potential class of women returning to the rank and file.[36]

In October 1979, AFA filed a motion with the U.S. District Court for the Northern District of Illinois, Eastern Division, to intervene in the case to represent the interests of the present working flight attendants. It also moved to file a cross claim against United to further protect the working flight attendants. On April 28, 1980, the court granted the motion to intervene.[37]

A trial was held in May 1981 to assess the effects reinstatement of the class would have on working flight attendants and United. By this time, five hundred United flight attendants were on the streets on furlough because of the financial difficulties UAL experienced as a result of airline deregulation in 1978. The active line flight attendants had much

92

to lose if the seniority lists were increased by large numbers of former stewardesses. The potential size of the class varied from several hundred up to more than two thousand.

The Association of Flight Attendants took and, as of this writing, takes a strong position that no flight attendant within the *McDonald* class action suit should be returned to active status. United Airlines takes the position that they are not liable for the back pay and also emphasizes the effect on morale that seniority adjustments would create.

At the May 1981 trial, the union presented testimony of many flight attendants who described the severe effects reinstatement would have on the working flight attendants and the unfairness of such a remedy. The union posture was supported by economist Olivia Mitchell, who emphasized that there have been significant changes since the mid-1960s in the extent to which women remain in the labor force after marriage and concluded that it was extremely unlikely that most of the class members would have remained at United even had there not been a no-marriage rule. [38]

On January 8, 1982, federal district judge James Moran ruled that reinstatement of the *McDonald* class was unprecedented and the effects inequitable. Accordingly, the court awarded those class members who could establish that they left United involuntarily due to the no-marriage rule only the amount of seniority which they had when they left United in the 1960s. On average, this seniority was around one and a half years. This decision greatly reduced the negative effects on the working flight attendants.

The S & S Division representatives had sometimes been without their own members' support in their efforts to relax discrimination and often had little more than the intent of Title VII to sustain their efforts. The agreement made on November 7, 1968, with United Airlines reveals the difficulty of eliminating discrimination at the bargaining table: "The Company agrees that marriage will not disqualify a Stewardess from continuing in the employ of the Company as a Stewardess, but any Stewardess who shall hereafter become pregnant shall have her services with the Company permanently severed."[39] The union had sought maternity leaves for all stewardesses regardless of marital status.

Diane Robertson, negotiator for the union, testified to the difficulty of negotiating the marriage and maternity issues. She lamented, "It may seem like harsh language, but we were facing male negotiators from the company. One said, 'Single girls shouldn't get pregnant. In my day the man was the aggressor.'"[40]

United Airlines management had observed that, regardless of company procedures and social pressures, a number of women of childbearing age will become pregnant. To deal with this inconvenience, the company had developed unwritten procedures applied on an individual basis. The pregnant stewardess was often given a leave of absence and could return to active flight status on the condition that she gave up her baby for adoption.

A few women were able to avoid this cruelty. If a stewardess had a medical leave unrelated to a pregnancy, she could hide the pregnancy from the company; or a stewardess could agree to put her baby up for adoption and then keep her baby provided she was not found out. One flight attendant on the early San Francisco–Honolulu route had a child who was three years old before the mother was discovered and fired.[41] Flying the military airlift command (MAC) operation from San Francisco to Southeast Asia, one unmarried flight attendant found a way to keep her baby. She was able to conceal her pregnancy from the company by bidding her vacation to coincide with her delivery date. She was overly cautious and waited more than three years after policies were changed to reveal the existence of her child to the company. Other flight attendants coped with the harsh realities of the contractual language covering pregnancy by electing abortion.

In the late 1960s the best the union could negotiate was an automatic layoff for UAL stewardesses while they were pregnant. They would continue to accrue seniority and could return to their jobs after delivery. The agreement with UAL permitted the stewardesses three months off after the birth, with the option of requesting an extension of time off, if needed. This compulsory unpaid maternity leave was challenged by several flight attendants on United, including Linda Mortimer and Mioslawa Rosenfeld who lived in the state of New York. M. *Rosenfeld* v. *United Airlines* originated in 1974. In this union-sponsored case, the New York State Division of Human Rights found that UAL maternity policies violated state law and ordered United to permit flight attendants to fly for the first twenty-seven weeks of pregnancy. After unsuccessful appeals before the New York State courts, UAL petitioned the U.S. Supreme Court to review the case, but the court denied the petition.[42]

United, after its long and unsuccessful court battle with Rosenfeld—whose child was now almost ready to enter school—decided to institute a new systemwide maternity leave policy for flight attendants, which became effective in December 1978.[43] The policy provided, among other things, for the stewardess to use her accrued sick leave during the entire period of her pregnancy. With a physician's permission (reevaluated on a monthly basis), she could work through the twenty-seventh week of pregnancy, the period established by the *Rosenfeld* decision, or she could take an unpaid medical leave of absence. Combinations of paid sick leave, medical leave, and work status also became available to the pregnant flight attendant. There were some safeguards for the health of the stewardess and the safety of the public: for instance, a stewardess, immediately upon learning of her pregnancy, must obtain her physician's permission to continue flying.

Stewardesses on most other U.S. airlines did not enjoy the same maternity policies as those on United. A variety of policies and rules pertaining to pregnant stewardesses have resulted from the decisions issued in the complicated cases filed under Title VII. On September 3, 1980, the U.S. Court of Appeals for the Fourth Circuit, in a sharply divided opinion, agreed that Eastern Airlines could ground a stewardess after the thirteenth week of pregnancy.[44] As late as January 6, 1981, the U.S. Court of Appeals for the Ninth Circuit ruled that Pan American World Airways may continue to ground flight attendants as soon as they learn they are pregnant. Although the court concluded Pan Am's policy was justified, it remanded for further consideration the question of when a flight attendant may return to work after childbirth and whether she may accrue seniority during maternity leave.[45]

Litigation on behalf of the stewardess did not go unnoticed. The *Honolulu Advertiser* published an article titled "Stews Got Pregnant and Lawyers Got Fat," explaining the $2.7 million settlement for 260 American Airlines stewardesses involved in an eight-year class action suit.[46] By 1974 nineteen of the S & S Division's twenty carriers had filed EEOC charges on maternity issues, weight issues, or both.[47] As the collective bargaining and legal pressures intensified against the airlines, a glaring example of disparate treatment of the sexes was needed to convince the courts of inequities.

In the 1960s, the airlines hired females almost exclusively for the job of flight attendant. American corporations have historically tended to promote reliance on women in certain occupations because females have usually provided cheap but educated labor. The airline industry capitalized on this tradition by initially hiring women nurses, steeped in the practice of nurturing, to provide extra care to airline customers. Sexist labeling, from the original sky girls to stewardesses and hostesses, undoubtedly helped to maintain the sexist employment policies of the air carriers.[48]

The most notable exceptions to these practices were UAL's Hawaiian stewards, whose ethnic characteristics were used as marketing attractions in much the same manner as the stewardesses' sexual characteristics and who performed the same job as regular stewardesses on the same flights. The stewards had always been permitted to marry, to have children, and to retain their position as stewards. These rights had been denied to stewardesses on the same Hawaiian operation. While some women had been removed from schedule for failure to maintain weight according to United's weight-height charts, weight control had not been enforced with the stewards.

Most Title VII lawsuits involving United Airlines pointed out the disparate treatment of the Hawaiian stewards and stewardesses, but the company claims of the stewards' ability to create a Hawaiian atmosphere persuaded some courts.[49] Then *Diaz v. Pan American World Airways, Inc.* challenged Pan American's policy of hiring only females as flight attendants. Diaz had made application for the job and was turned down because he was male. The court proceedings of the *Diaz* case provide a blueprint of the airlines' pattern of utilization of traditional female roles. The Air Transport Association (ATA), an organization supported mainly by the air carriers, embarked on an impressive and calculated defense of the practice of hiring women as flight attendants. Immediate economic motives for the airline industry's support of Pan American in the defense against the *Diaz* case were apparent: a convincing justification of discriminatory practices could influence the demands for reparations from flight attendants.

Pan American claimed that the overall performance of females in the job of flight attendant was superior to males, submitted a survey that indicated "passenger preference" for stewardesses, and offered testimony from a psychiatrist and a psychologist to support their assertions. The claim of superior performance by women in the job of flight attendant was based on Pan Am's own experience of hiring mixed male-female cabin crews. The allegedly scientific survey had been made by Opinion Research Corporation of Princeton, New Jersey, as requested by the Air Transport Association.

In his testimony, psychiatrist Eric Berne explained why airline passengers prefer to be served by females. Berne described the environment of an airplane as a "sealed enclave" that creates three typical passenger emotional states: apprehension, boredom, and excitement. It was Berne's opinion that females, because of their psychological relationships to persons of both sexes, are better able to deal with each of these three psychological states. Explaining that many male passengers would subconsciously resent a male flight attendant, whom they might perceive as more masculine than they, and respond negatively to a male flight attendant perceived as less masculine, Berne believed that male passengers would generally feel more masculine and thus more at ease in the presence of a young female attendant. There was no challenge to Berne's qualifications as an expert, and the court found a considerable part of his testimony persuasive.

The airlines moved on to introduce more expert advice. Raymond A. Katzell, chairman of the department of psychology at New York University, offered testimony on the difficulty in finding male flight attendants who possessed traits of "femininity." Testifying that while some men possessed one or more of the "feminine" qualities (e.g., benevolence, genuine interest in the comfort of others, lack of perceived aggressiveness), he stated that only infrequently would the airlines find a man possessing each of these traits to at least as high a degree as the average woman. The court opinion described Katzell's testimony as "impressive."

The U.S. District Court, Southern District of Florida, determined that Pan American had not unlawfully discriminated on the grounds of sex under section 703 of Title VII when it did not hire applicant Diaz. In an ironic twist, the court also pointed out that Diaz was not qualified for the position of flight attendant because he was, at age thirty, too old.[50] The U.S. Court of Appeals for the Fifth Circuit, in reversing the district court in *Diaz* held that sex was merely tangential to the business of the airline—transportation—and did not meet the business-necessity test dictated by the court.[51] In February 1972, United added to its domestic operations three stewards whom they had hired earlier for the Hawaiian operations and then subsequently furloughed; in April UAL hired its first male flight attendant specifically for domestic operations.

By the early 1970s, the quarreling over whether sex was a bona fide occupational qualification for the position of flight attendant was becoming a moot issue. The courts were upholding the EEOC opinions that it was not. In the meantime, unions representing flight attendants attacked other discriminatory policies, including the grounding of stewardesses mainly between the ages of thirty-two and thirty-five and the application of restrictive weight and appearance guidelines.

At United the "qualifications" for stewardesses had for years been drummed into applicants as well as line flight attendants. Mary O'Connor's partial list of job standards illustrates that to the traditional sex discrimination were added those based on age and race: "Are you between twenty and twenty-seven years of age? Are you between 5'2" and 5'8"? Do you weigh not more than one hundred and thirty-eight pounds in proportion to your height? Are you single? . . . Are your hands soft and white? . . . Are you a R.N.? Have you a college degree? Have you had two years of college?"[52] Although breaking the hiring barrier on UAL in 1963, black women undoubtedly discovered additional forms of discrimination that applied only to women employed as stewardesses.

Throughout most of the 1960s grooming rules for United stewardesses were paramilitary. Girdles were to be worn, and periodic touch checks were made by some supervisors. Nail polish and lipstick were required, and the colors were selected from an approved list. Hair could not extend over the uniform blouse collar and could not be worn in an upswept fashion. Dyeing of hair or bleaching of hair was prohibited. Straightening of hair for black women was acceptable, but Afro, corn-row, and braided hairstyles were taboo. Hats and gloves were to be worn at all times. Part of the routine flight duties included appearance checks by the flight attendant herself to ensure that her appearance was not disheveled. Hosiery with runs was expected to be replaced by an extra pair of stockings carried as important equipment. During the early 1960s white uniform blouses were often checked for perspiration stains. The flight attendant's job entails a lot of bending, walking, pushing, and pulling. Stewardesses did run stockings, and some did sweat. The appearance regulations for the airlines read as though the hard work aspects of the stewardess job were to be covered up.

Partially to further monitor appearance, United created an appearance counselor's job for the various domiciles. Stewardesses were invited to come into the offices to try out new makeup and hairstyles. Scales were added to some of the appearance rooms. At the Denver appearance room in the late 1960s, the practice of measuring the vital statistics of the new transfers into the domicile became common, and at one point the measuring was extended to all Denver-based stewardesses.

Some flight attendants did complain about what they considered unreasonable appearance requirements. By 1973, the S & S Division had filed EEOC complaints against sixteen airlines charging that weight standards were arbitrary and discriminatory. In addition, *Air Line Pilots Association, Int'l* v. *United Air Lines, Inc.* was filed in district court in New York.

Not a few United stewardesses observed that the Hawaiian stewards were exempt from the practice of weight checks, and had been since 1949 when they were first hired. In 1972 the company drew the stewards into a weight guideline program, which was more generous with weight exceptions than the one for women. Even with the more flexible weight limitations, many of the 184 Hawaiian stewards were outraged that restrictive weight guidelines were being enforced on them. One steward complained that he had been hired as a Hawaiian and now the company expected him to be a "thin-hipped Norwegian."

In 1978, three stewards, Eric Yamaguchi, Dave Morton, and Mel Melvin, journeyed from Hawaii to New York to testify in the class action suit against United. Although they had not suffered suspensions they gallantly joined the women who had been the objects of discipline for carrying more pounds than the company deemed acceptable. The court's decision on June 12, 1979, ruled that United discriminated against female flight attendants in the application and enforcement of its weight program: "United's enforcement of its weight program has not been even-handed, but instead has discriminated against females both in the frequency and severity of discipline imposed." The court concluded that the height-weight standards themselves did not violate Title VII and that while United's weight exception policies discriminatorily favored Hawaiian stewards, that discrimination was justified by "special circumstances," and so did not violate Title VII.

The decision enjoined UAL from discriminating on the basis of sex in enforcement of its weight standards, including any discipline or penalties; awarded back pay to each female flight attendant terminated, suspended, or removed from schedule for weight since March 24, 1972, and interest at the rate of 6 percent on all back pay; ordered reinstatement of all female flight attendants terminated for weight since March 24, 1972, return of currently suspended or removed flight attendants, and the purging of flight attendant records pertaining to weight discipline. United would pay all attorney's fees and litigation expenses. United did not appeal the case.[53]

Other "fat" cases, however, were not decided in favor of the flight attendants. Continental Airlines flight attendants were denied their suit of discrimination in 1978 by U.S. District Court judge Jesse W. Curtis when he dismissed a legal action for weight that was initiated in 1972: "It is now well established that federal sex discrimination laws do not forbid employers to set appearance standards," he said. "These are the kinds of choices which allow some businesses to succeed while others fail. . . ."[54] This case is now on appeal.

Just as the airlines had in mind an ideal weight for their stewardesses, they had in mind an ideal age. During the 1950s and 1960s, stewardesses over thirty-two or thirty-five were fired by some carriers. American Airlines was the first carrier to be successful in grounding stewardesses on account of age. When the issue first arose in the early 1950s the ALSSA union cried "propwash" to the idea that stewardesses over thirty were too old to fly, and on some carriers, such as United, the union was able to hold off a provision for early retirement.

United, however, implemented its own method of dealing with what it considered the age problem. During the mid-1960s stewardesses hiring on would be asked to sign a form agreeing that they would quit or transfer to a ground job when they reached the age of thirty-two. One Norwegian new hire exlaimed, "This is the craziest thing I have seen!"and would not sign the agreement. United took no action against her, but she recalled, "My teacher at the training center explained that it was something that the company wished them to do."[55]

The airlines' defense of their age requirement was that the older stewardesses lacked the strength, stamina, and enthusiasm required for the position. Their arguments were not accepted by the EEOC, and in *Dodd* v. *American Airlines, Inc.*, the findings showed that a reasonable cause existed to believe that the rule violated Title VII.[56] By the 1970s most U.S. carriers had given up on the age requirement, leaving some international carriers, including Japan Airlines and Sabena, to deal with the troublesome process of forcing stewardesses to retire while in their thirties.

Unions representing flight attendants were active in filing complaints and commencing litigation immediately after the implementation of the Title VII. As the court cases began to drag on at the various levels of the nation's courts, the S & S Division emerged as one of the more persistent unions representing stewardesses in the pursuit of class action suits against employers. There are several reasons for this development. By 1970 the S & S Division, under ALPA, represented twenty-two carriers, the most for any flight attendant union, and thus, more and varied discriminatory requirements were leveled by employers at its members. Second, as vice president of ALPA's S & S Division, Kelly Rueck threw heavy support behind the women's issues, soliciting the support of J. J. O'Donnell, ALPA's new president, and attacking airline policies on behalf of the entire flight attendant group.[57]

Rueck's strong position on women's issues was not always accepted by all members and officers of the S & S Division. Her course was one of some risk. Many Americans were not yet aware of the subordinate status of women, and within the stewardess ranks there was the same lag in awareness. Many stewardesses agreed with company policies, and it was not unusual to hear such comments as, "Well, I don't think we should be married and fly; we knew when we were hired that we couldn't be married," "I think the company has a right to have weight check—some of the stewardesses will be too fat to fit into the jumpseats," "I don't think men should be hired for the job," and "It's not fair that pregnant women can take leaves, accrue seniority, then return to work—some of them don't need the money, anyway."

Throughout the 1960s there was some thread of officer continuity within the S & S Division. But the company attitude toward the stewardess union was usually one of disinterest, and according to Diane Robertson, a union officer during that period, "Union representatives were often viewed by management as frustrated women who had failed to fulfill themselves with the 'proper' goals of marriage and family." Although the stewardesses had the right to bargain collectively, they were not a threatening force and "were treated as some sort of nuisance although as an organization with which, under the law, the company had to deal at times."

Robertson pointed out that the company had no reason to take the stewardesses seriously because of their short tenure and because most stewardesses were not much interested in the union. The rank and file's attitude toward unionism often undercut their officers' effectiveness: "the 'girls', as they were called at that time, would often say: 'Well, my Daddy hates unions. . . .' Many of them had their minds on finding themselves an appropriate husband so that they could get on with their lives. This attitude drastically affected our union strength."[58]

The small number of UAL Hawaiian stewards viewed the union quite differently. The number of stewards was eight in 1949 and slowly climbed to only one hundred forty-five by 1975; during the same period the UAL stewardess ranks swelled from several hundred to approximately seven thousand. Nevertheless, the stewards had generally become union members and good union workers. The predominantly female union group was often represented at various labor functions by the United stewards.

Throughout the 1960s it was mainly the S & S Division leaders who resolutely continued to build union strength. Still under ALPA, the

S & S Division was working to create a better national union structure. Both the pilots and the stewardesses had been able to work with the complicated percentage vote-casting system, calculated according to membership, to elect their high-ranking officers. Although there were some rumblings on both sides, as long as the pilots outnumbered the stewardesses, which they did in the 1960s, there seemed little threat that the stewardesses would seriously attempt to solidify support for an election of a specific presidential candidate. The power law with the pilots. At the conventions the women who represented the S & S Division were secluded, a practice not unlike the segregation of women in medieval churches.

The ALPA S & S Division conventions of the late 1960s were the calm before the storm. The stewardess rank and file had undergone enormous changes with the relaxation of discrimination, modified agency shop agreements, and a resurgence of militant feminism, which had been largely dormant since the 1920s. [59] The industry's preparation for the jumbo jets was swelling the flight attendant ranks to unprecedented levels. The pilots were among the first to notice that, numerically and psychologically, the Stewards and Stewardesses Division was becoming a powerful and threatening force.

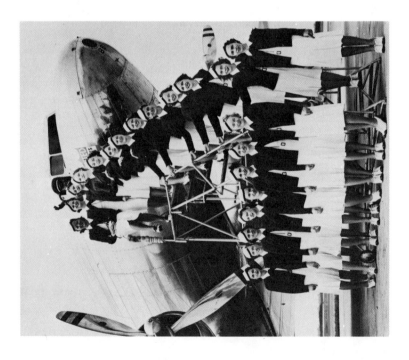

Facing page, left: A 1938 publicity photo documents the airlines' longtime use of the flight attendants as a marketing attraction. (Photo courtesy of United Airlines.) *Right:* Rigid grooming standards of the 1950s ensured that the flight attendants lived up to the fresh, girl-next-door image the airlines used in their advertising. (Photo courtesy of Frontier Airlines.)

Above: A negotiations committee for Flying Tiger caucuses at AFA's national headquarters, 1982. *Right:* Linda Puchala, president of AFA, speaking at a press conference held by the National Organization of Women to spur on ratification of the Equal Rights Amendment, 1982. (Photo courtesy of Association of Flight Attendants.)

5
The "Stewardess Problem"

In the early 1960s pilots had referred to the "stewardess problem"; ten years later it had become simply "the problem."[1] Confrontations over affiliation status and election of ALPA officers had been interrupted by short periods of relative calm, but by the 1970s the renewed interest in feminism quickened the pilots' anxieties. While the twenty-seven-thousand–member pilot division was more than double the eleven-thousand-member S & S Division,[2] there was a very real threat that with the increasing number of flight attendants hired to staff the jumbo jets the stewardesses would outnumber the pilots. Under the ALPA constitution and bylaws, the S & S Division flight attendants could support a candidate and influence the election of ALPA's president. Many pilots wanted the stewardesses and stewards out of the union, and they wanted them out immediately: even those who wanted to maintain the close relationship saw a need for reform of ALPA's constitution and bylaws.[3]

Because ALPA had the constitutional authority to dissolve the S & S Division and be rid of these annoying and threatening members, it may seem strange that the pilots were even continuing to bother with the stewardesses. The obvious explanation that the pilots put up with these women to keep them under their thumb is too simplistic. By the early 1970s, about half the unionized flight attendants had a home within ALPA. For the pilots to eliminate the S & S Division seemed inappropriate to many. If the all-male pilot union pushed the stewardess members out on a limb, it could cause negative publicity. The pilots had much to lose.

The public has traditionally held the pilots in high esteem. With a conservative image and no scandals to rock its foundation, ALPA's leadership had been strong and respected. Perhaps even more important, the government had, until the Airline Deregulation Act of 1978, been a watchdog over the entire airline industry. Taking pride in its dedication to democratic ideals, the pilot union was being closely watched to see how it would deal with the stewardess problem. Its solution would be analyzed by the AFL-CIO, the airline industry and its unions, and advocates for women's rights. To protect their members in the S & S Division, the ALPA leaders would need to pay attention to their previous commitments, the present economic health of their union, and the future goodwill of all parties involved.

ALPA itself had undergone leadership changes during the 1960s. The union had three levels of leadership: the presidency, providing strong, central leadership; the board of directors, composed of elected officers from the local levels; and the Executive Central Committee, comprising five regional vice presidents plus three national officers.[4] The board of directors could change this structure by mandate, but as yet had not exercised that power.

Clarence Sayen, president during the creation of the S & S Division, resigned as ALPA's leader in 1962. He had intentionally stepped down at mid-term to enable an election for his successor. Sayen was a polished, articulate young man with an academic bent, and his image pleased many ALPA members. His successor, Charles Ruby, was a hard-working old-timer who had been a chief pilot with National Airlines. In many ways a sharp contrast to Sayen, he became subject to recall efforts, but these were thwarted. Ruby managed to hang on to the presidency on one occasion by casting a vote for himself. The power struggle within ALPA would continue into the early 1970s. While members of the S & S Division could not be candidates for the position of the presidency, they could exercise a block vote to sway an election, and hence become kingmakers. There were some pilots who would not hesitate to exploit this potential. Pushed to the extreme, the stewardesses themselves might try to challenge the structure and force reforms that would enable them to elect a stewardess as president of ALPA.

It was very important to the pilots that they elect a pilot president; they did not want their union to be led by a flight attendant. In the late 1960s the recall of Ruby again became an issue, and during the 1968 board of directors meeting some pilots made an attempt to draw the stewardess delegates into the politicking. While the stewardesses refrained from casting block votes to sway the election, the potential power of the fast-growing S & S Division did not go unnoticed by the pilot officers. [5]

Ruby was approaching sixty, and under ALPA's constitution he could not run for reelection. Many potential pilot candidates emerged. At least ten pilots were seriously campaigning for the office at the biennial board of directors meeting held in November 1970 in Miami. With the S & S Division again refraining from a block vote, J. J. O'Donnell, a popular Eastern pilot, emerged the winner on the fifteenth ballot; after two days of roll-call voting he received a 59 percent majority. [6] O'Donnell had not wanted the flight attendants to be involved in the voting processes for the presidency.

The pilots had refrained from exercising votes for the S & S Division's highest office, vice president of ALPA, much in the same way that the flight attendants did not vote for a presidential candidate. The highest office for the S & S Division was won by stewardess Kelly Rueck on the first count. [7] A native of Alabama, Rueck had started flying for United in 1964. She commenced her union career with the local council in Denver, and by the end of the 1960s she had been elected to the highest union office for stewardesses on UAL. Rueck put a high value on education and training of officers and encouraged the group to "stand on their own feet." [8]

Two days after their elections, O'Donnell and Rueck met to discuss the organizational structure of the union. The prohibitions against stewardesses and stewards holding ALPA's highest office were to be explored, among other organizational problems, by an S & S Division study committee. [9]

Rueck had a keen sense of the status of the steward and stewardess group and began efforts to strengthen its position. Described as a very strong-willed woman, Rueck had locked horns with J. J. O'Donnell on several occasions;[10] however, many contemporary officers and flight attendants agreed that she was headed in the right direction in paving the way for independence of the stewards and stewardesses.[11] A high-ranking ALPA official explained that O'Donnell tried to maintain a working relationship with the flight attendants and that "Rueck understood the politics of the pilots probably as well as the pilots."[12] Maintaining an open-door policy, Rueck had started the practice of convening the executive board (comprised of the highest elected officers from each carrier, the master executive council chairpersons), which had no power for overall policy but could provide a forum for exchange of ideas; the de facto power of the group was its influence with local council chairpersons, who, in turn, formed the board of directors.

Rueck's formidable leadership of the S & S Division, undoubtedly added to the frustrations of the pilots. In contrast to earlier confrontations, the pilot union began to play rough, albeit by very subtle rules. There were only two full-time S & S Division representatives working in the new Washington, D.C., headquarters ALPA had moved to by 1970—Rueck and department head of safety Delfina Mott. Mott worked closely with the ALPA representatives on safety matters and had devoted nearly a decade to issues of cabin safety. Government agencies, some aircraft manufacturers, and other interested parties had begun to solicit Mott's opinions, and her views were sought for congressional hearings on airline safety. While she was becoming a valuable spokeswoman and her working relationship with ALPA was amicable, she believed that within the union she was becoming a political symbol and the object of political infighting.

Abruptly, Mott was moved from the second-floor office she shared with the ALPA safety staff to the seventh floor. Her new office had been a storage closet and featured poor lighting, no window, and a location behind a noisy elevator shaft. She registered complaints with O'Donnell and Rueck, as well as OSHA. The battle continued for months, and in an unusually drastic move, she relocated her office into the women's room, which was on the same floor. Eventually, J. J. O'Donnell paid a visit to her closet office, but the problem was not resolved until the 1973 convention when O'Donnell announced he had given orders for Mott's office to be moved to a more suitable area.[13]

This incident illustrates the limitations on the ways the pilot union could display displeasure with the S & S Division. Because the division was highly decentralized and structured along autonomous and democratic lines, its officers had little contact with the pilot union.

Meanwhile, the S & S Division's newly hired law firm solicited the U.S. Department of Labor to review ALPA's umbrella status. An associate solicitor for the department pointed out that the first conflict with the Landrum-Griffin Act concerned the restriction on eligibility for the office of president to members of the Pilot Division. Further, since the offices of secretary and treasurer of the Pilot Division were assigned general responsibilities on behalf of the entire association, all members must be eligible for those offices.[14] The review also included a suggestion that the constitutions be amended to avoid costly and disruptive litigation.[15]

For the next three years the issue would take up the energies of the boards of directors for both the pilots and flight attendants. The problem was dealt with at the usual meeting in 1972, again in a special meeting in June 1973, and yet again in another special meeting in October 1973. Throughout this period, the regular meetings of the executive boards for both groups, as well as specially called meetings, also dealt almost exclusively with the problem.

At the June 1973 board of directors meeting, feelings ran high. Several proposals for autonomy were considered, but the two-thirds vote required from the S & S Division was not obtained. While tensions at the convention were not unlike those of the 1960 meeting when a stewardess union had been compromised into the S & S Division, by 1973 the pilots were in more general agreement that they had to be rid of these women. There were fewer platitudes about democracy and quotations from the founding fathers of the nation. Whereas in 1960 ALPA's leaders had gone to some length to contain the stewardesses within the union, now they were going to do whatever it took to get these women out of the internal structure of ALPA.

On September 13, 1973, a special board of directors meeting was called for "debate and voting" on alternative courses of action. In May 1973, the pilot executive board had endorsed the pilot committee proposals and reminded the members that they were faced with the necessity of electing national officers in November 1974. Both the pilots and flight attendants feared that the more radical groups would attempt to force the issue by trying to nominate and to elect a member of the S & S Division president of ALPA. If that happened, the pilots would almost certainly invoke the dissolution provision and eliminate the S & S Division, and the Department of Labor would undoubtedly step in then to void the elections and hold its own. In October 1973, the S & S Division board of directors again elected to maintain the status quo.[16]

Protests had been pouring in from the pilots. A telex from TWA announced, "TWA pilots are dismayed by lack of progress on the S & S question; since timeliness is a primary consideration . . . accordingly we support any plan which you and the committee propose if it is positive action now."[17] A telex from Eastern Airlines' pilot members was less patient: "It is the opinion of the MEC [Master Executive Council] that action is long overdue to bring the association back under the absolute control of the pilots."[18] The most scathing attack came from a member of the pilot study committee on the problem. In a telex to J. J. O'Donnell, George Berg charged that the vice president for the S & S Division, Kelly Rueck, and the majority of the S & S study committee members were attempting to extract an unreasonable subsidy from the ALPA Pilot Division. Rejecting the retention of the S & S Division in any fashion, he called for actions that would request immediate payment for all outstanding S & S Division debts and would eliminate all further credit to the S & S Division.[19]

Kelly Rueck had the task of reconciling the several points of view within the flight attendant ranks. Some members and leaders wanted a complete break with the pilots; others were content with the status quo; and a sizable number wanted a new autonomy that would be acceptable to both pilots and flight attendants. Some of the same political elements that had deeply split the rank and file during the 1960 reaffiliation were again present. According to Rueck, "The United group, with more union experience than some of the others, remained largely in the middle-of-the-road."[20] The leaders for some of the smaller carriers, who were still very dependent on pilots and on the paternalism of the companies, were split on the issue. Attendants on other small carriers, most notably Continental Airlines, were militant in their desire for a showdown with the pilots.[21] An attempt to force the pilots to open their union to the future election of a stewardess to the presidency would, in fact, sever the S & S Division from ALPA.

An ALPA pilot officer who worked with the study committee that functioned from 1972 to 1974 believed that the pilots were not so concerned about the flight attendants who were activists in the women's movement as they were about the women in the S & S Division "who could determine who their president was going to be."[22] As the count-down began for the 1974 board of directors meeting at which election of ALPA's president would take place, the differences magnified.

When the push for a flight attendant charter began in 1960, nearly all the flight attendants were organized within ALPA. TWU held bargaining rights for the handful from Pan American. By the early 1970s, however, the situation was markedly different. Many of the S & S Division leaders believed that with only around fourteen thousand of the flight attendants within their union it could not become independent unless the fifteen thousand from ALSSA joined in their effort. But the timing was unfortunate, and the ALSSA group would not enter into the fracas until later in the decade. Also, analyzing their financial situation, some members and leaders of the S & S Division determined that they could not on their own provide collective bargaining, organizing, grievance processing, and administrative services to their members.[23]

The three unions the study committee considered as alternatives to ALPA were the Air Line Stewards and Stewardesses Association (ALSSA), to which many had belonged before its 1960 split from ALPA; the International Association of Machinists and Aerospace Workers (IAMAW); and the International Brotherhood of Teamsters (IBT). Additionally, the S & S Division had solicited background information from the Brotherhood of Railway, Airline, and Steamship Clerks, Freight Handlers, Express and Station Employees (BRAC) and from the Air Line Employees Association (ALEA), affiliated with ALPA. The study committee made no recommendations on any of the unions to the board of directors. Rather, it presented a structure of each for evaluation and comparison to their current arrangement with ALPA.

Some members of the board were incensed that the committee even eyed the Teamsters and ALSSA as alternatives because the S & S Division had experienced raids from both groups.[24] Conversely, the S & S Division through ALPA, had made some raids of their own against these groups; the raids against the Teamsters were "open house" because that group was not an AFL-CIO union, and after ALSSA's break with the pilot union, the usual no-raid provisions for AFL-CIO unions did not prevail with either ALPA or the TWU. Initially, George Meany declared that the TWU's charter to the dissident ALSSA group constituted a raid. Somewhat tardily, in 1963 ALPA pursued the jurisdictional claim through AFL-CIO's neutral hearing board but backed off when it recognized the elasticity of the AFL-CIO's constitutional prohibition of raiding. Thus, the TWU and the ALPA had been able to attempt to raid each other's flight attendant membership with some regularity;[25] the flight attendants on Northwest, for example, have the dubious distinction of having been members of ALSSA with ALPA, ALSSA with TWU, the S & S Division of ALPA, the Association of Flight Attendants, and the Teamsters within little more than a decade.

Some of the steward and stewardess leadership understood that the effective and efficient bureaucracy, which had been built up within the pilot union, was highly desirable for their group. The field offices, conveniently located in the domicile cities for ALPA's carriers, had been shared by the S & S Division; this arrangement had provided the organizational structure that enabled dissemination of information, contract administration, training sessions, and administrative services. A working relationship with the pilot union had another advantage the flight attendants might not want to lose, the essential legal assistance of ALPA lawyers and its counsel hired on retainer.

Many of the S & S Division representatives had turned down the last of the many pilot proposals because of the provisions for staff and services (there had been six official and many more unofficial proposals rejected). Consequently, after the October 10, 1973, special board of directors meeting Rueck and O'Donnell met to discuss the problem areas, and as a result, the pilots came forward with an improved offer that contained an affiliation agreement, changes for the constitution and bylaws, and a more comprehensive administrative agreement. The administrative agreement provided an arrangement for a staff and other essentials for a period of five years, including services worth $100,000 each year; use of the ALPA staff at least at the current level of services; free use of the home office, parking spaces, WATS lines, and telex through 1975; continuation of use of the field offices at not more than $100 a month each; representation at the AFL-CIO conventions; a process for any disputes concerning the agreement; no back debt to the pilots; a procedure for obtaining new or expanded services; assistance in obtaining a line of credit or loans if necessary; and assistance in training programs for negotiating committee members, system board members, and administrative assistants. [26]

The affiliation agreement provides for each union to govern its own affairs, establish and implement its own policy, and remain fiscally and administratively independent. Neither organization can seek control over the affairs of the other or be accountable for the actions or obligations of the other, its officers, or members. All dues of the AFA members are paid directly to the Association of Flight Attendants and all ALPA property remains under ALPA ownership. Full-time employees of AFA are entitled to participate in ALPA's fringe benefit program. The affiliation will remain in effect until terminated or modified by mutual agreement of ALPA and AFA. At any time after six months notice to each other, the affiliation of AFA and ALPA may be dissolved by a two-thirds vote by either AFA's or ALPA's board of directors. [27]

In November 1973, ballots were sent to the S & S Division's board of directors, each member of which represented a local council in the voting. The final tally was 10,709 in favor of the proposal and 1,786 against; thus, the two-thirds necessary affirmative vote was achieved. The approved proposals were contingent on the National Mediation Board's recognition of the new union, the Association of Flight Attendants, as the bargaining representative for the former S & S Division members. "Indeed," the pilots' report cautioned, "without such recognition, it is doubtful that the pilots will have achieved their major objective in seeking the restructuring—a lawful structure under which they can elect their own President without joint participation by the cabin attendants. . . ."[28]

Within six months after the study began, the National Mediation Board, on December 4, 1974, proposed a ratification procedure. One of the NMB's chief designers of the procedure was Rowland K. Quinn, who had led another group of flight attendants through disaffiliation with ALPA ten years earlier, and was now executive secretary of the NMB. Quinn's letter to the parties, which shows a professional detachment from the same problems he once was so much a part of, proposed that if a simple majority of one vote more than 50 percent of the flight attendants on each carrier formerly represented by the S & S Division of ALPA voted to transfer bargaining representation from ALPA to AFA, the autonomous and independent status could be accomplished.[29] Over the next six years, the referenda were returned to the National Mediation Board. Allegheny (now USAir) was the first to approve AFA in 1975,[30] and by 1978 fifteen of the sixteen carriers represented by AFA had voted to make the Association of Flight Attendants their official representative. Western Airlines completed the AFA roster vote on March 30, 1979.[31]

During the interim, ALPA and AFA implemented all aspects of the affiliation agreement other than the formal transfer of bargaining rights, and AFA continued collective bargaining on an independent basis.

At the end of 1975, Rueck resigned as president, effective January 16, 1976, and relinquished the office to her successor, Pat Robertson of Piedmont Airlines, saying "No organization provides a finer system of representation for its members than AFA. The democracy and member participation is not found in most labor organizations because it is considered too cumbersome and costly. . . ."[32]

In its first years of existence, the AFA experienced a period of staggering growth. In 1969 the S & S Division represented ten thousand members, and by 1974 the number had reached twenty thousand. During the same period, the average annual salary of AFA members had climbed from $5,000 to approximately $10,000, and the average length of service had changed from one and a half years to about six years. Simultaneously, the economic recession of 1970 and 1971 had prompted aircraft groundings and mass schedule reductions within the airline industry. In this period of belt-tightening, some twenty-two thousand airline workers were unemployed, and by early 1974 approximately seventeen thousand airline employees were still on the furlough lists. Flight attendants had survived the cutbacks; few were furloughed. Normal attrition helped to alleviate the surplus pressures from their already lean ranks. [33]

Business for the unions representing flight attendants was intensified. Protracted negotiations and strikes were straining the AFA budget, and the expenditures for negotiations and arbitration soared. According to former secretary-treasurer Fran Hay, the last six months of 1975 were very difficult: "We really did not know if we would make it; we began to cut back and we applied strict accountability for expenditures. . . . I received the name of 'Scrooge.' It was a matter of survival."[34] The newly formed union had no time for the luxury of carefully planning their future. Kelly Rueck had acknowledged the uncertainties when she stated, "I believe we will measure our future progress in days."[35]

6
A Women's Union

Most airline managements had not perceived the effects of the revival of feminism. The companies continued to market their sky girls in hard-hitting campaigns. National Airlines advertised, "I'm Cheryl, fly me," and Continental Airlines, in newspapers and on radio, claimed, "We really move our tail for you."[1] On Continental, whose marketing tactics sometimes appalled even its competitors, the management had used Playboy bunnies as stewardesses for one week in 1975. But the gimmick failed because "nobody wanted a bunny on their armrest at eight o'clock in the morning."[2] Calling this kind of advertising degrading, Kelly Rueck warned that it might result in "a spontaneous loss of enthusiasm by airline stewardesses."[3] Danny Todd, chairman of the National Transportation Safety Board, noted that flight attendants have "been looked at by marketing people as their personal prerogative."[4]

A similar attitude toward the stewardesses prevailed at many of their bargaining tables, and the women negotiating the 1974 agreement for United Airlines flight attendants began the process of breaking the traditions of social, political, and economic discrimination against women. According to negotiator Nancy Williams, "Everything was going for us if we took advantage of it. The timing was right."[5]

The lower court decisions on Title VII were beginning to be over-turned, and it was clear that sex would not be a bona fide occupational qualification for flight attendants. United Airlines cautiously began to include males as regular flight attendants. In February 1972, UAL added three furloughed Hawaiian operations stewards to the domestic route roster, and in April 1972, graduated its first male flight attendants hired specifically for its domestic operations. Negotiator Williams believed that because males were joining the ranks, pressures to improve conditions would increase. This presumption was based on a belief that men were generally not expected to accept the same working conditions and salaries as women.

Along with Williams, Susan Rohde and Sue Bianchi were elected by the United AFA master executive council to negotiate the 1974 amendments to the 1972 White Book contractual agreement. In keeping with the policy of AFA, all three women were flight attendants with UAL. Their negotiating team included Mary Lyn Moseley, the elected master executive council chairperson for AFA on United Airlines, and negotiator Joan Prince from the home office. Although experience as a union officer was not required, two of the elected negotiators, Susan Rohde and Sue Bianchi, had served as local council officers. Only Williams had not served in union office, but with thirteen years as a stewardess, she had the most work experience.[6]

Moseley and the three elected negotiators attended training sessions led by John Sloan, senior staff associate at the AFL-CIO Labor Studies Center. Emphasizing strategy and tactics, Sloan taught them perhaps the most essential aspect of negotiating—the importance of getting along with each other as a team. Rohde confirmed that "we would later learn how important the psychological training had been. . . ." Sloan also explained the significance of having one team member become the speaker for the group. In that way, fewer mistakes would be made, and caucusing of their group, which would ensure that all subjects were thoroughly reviewed before the bargaining sessions, would be required on an ongoing basis. If disagreements among the union negotiating members surfaced during sessions, the team was advised to pass notes to each other or to call recesses.

The negotiating team had done its homework and presented its opener for approval of the AFA United master executive council on June 25, 1974. "The council was initially very supportive," recalled Rohde, and it voted its approval.[7] The proposal for the amendment of the 1972 contract contained more than three hundred issues. In addition to the usual items on compensation, hours of work, working conditions, and a procedure for the orderly settlement of disputes, there were other major redresses to bring to the attention of the corporation. The low value the company seemed to place on the stewardesses' service had to be challenged. "Our contractual agreements would be meaningless," Williams asserted, "without the respect and equality that was due us as working women."[8]

The company was unprepared for them. At their first meeting with the company, spokeswoman Rohde announced, "We are going to be treated equally." Knowing that historically the company had negotiated with unions on its administrative terms and its property, the women said, "We desire to meet one week in San Francisco and one week in Chicago." The company officials were astonished. A company negotiator left the room and discussed the problem with other company officials. Returning, the negotiator replied that they could meet the next week in San Francisco and the following week in Chicago. The union team suspected that they were being temporarily humored. They were correct. The same negotiations regarding meeting places were necessary every week. The women prevailed, and the team became a transient negotiating team.

The union team insisted on written, as opposed to oral, proposals. While the company often turned in handwritten proposals, the union team turned in typewritten proposals. They were trying to be accepted as equal to the company negotiators. Although they believed they were more professional than the company's team, instead of achieving acceptance as equals, they were becoming branded as radicals by the company.

The sex discrimination barrier loomed so large that the team came to see that problem as inseparable from the other issues being negotiated. "As negotiations went on," Rohde reported, "we found out that sex discrimination went hand in hand with our inability to force the officials to deal with us as equal partners."[9]

The United negotiating team included women, but the union negotiators viewed the company female negotiators as tokens. They were from local levels of flight attendant management, and while they fulfilled the function of being part of the company's committee, some union negotiators believed that they had little clout.

According to company negotiator Chuck Thomson, who joined the company team about a year after negotiations commenced, "United had never seen anything like it. The proposal looked like the New York telephone book. . . . The negotiators had completely rewritten the contract. I think their demands numbered over three hundred, and the costs were more than $250 million." It was the most costly opening proposal that United had ever seen by any union.

A number of sessions broke down because of the union team's perceptions of the company's manner of addressing them. "Procedures were very important to them," Thomson said, "I don't think that there would have been any way that we could have prepared for it; it was something that we had to go through as a learning experience. I am not sure that any experience anywhere else could have helped."[10]

During three lengthy lapses in talks, the union team took to the skies to conduct road shows for the rank and file. These meetings proved effective. "We had the power and the legal right to be the voice for the flight attendants," Williams said. "We had to educate them that they could be taken seriously; we had to teach them what we knew."[11] The negotiating team also placed articles on the progress of negotiations in the publication *Agenda*.

Meanwhile, the UAL master executive council that had elected the negotiations committee became deeply divided and harbored some doubts about the progress of the negotiations. The disruptive internal forces created arguments and forced elections. The negotiations committee was left intact, but four different master executive council chairpersons led the team during the period from the beginning of negotiations in the summer of 1974 to November 1975.

The negotiations committee was sensitive to how the company might perceive the politicking within the union. Rohde pointed out that the company had little to lose by dragging out negotiations because there was a possibility that the team could be worn down, the internal union divisions within the leadership ranks could bring the downfall of the negotiating team, or the rank and file could become impatient with the pace of negotiations.[12]

By February 1975, the union and company had gone into mediation under the jurisdiction of the National Mediation Board, and it was then that the company began an effort to communicate with the rank and file. The company believed that the union was being overzealous and overreacting in some of their proposals, and "we thought that we had an obligation as a company to let the flight attendants know what was going on . . . not to overthrow the union but to educate the union."[13]

The company began its program by sending a letter to all flight attendants, signed by the chairman of the board of United Airlines.[14] The union negotiators were outraged, but could do little to stop informational communication. Next, "informational" centers were set up throughout the UAL system so that management representatives could meet personally with flight attendants to provide information regarding the negotiations. Thomson discussed company motives: "On the line everything appeared to be going well. There were no big problems. There were no raids. We thought, 'What's going on here?' The average flight attendant seems to be happy. Corporate officers were flying all over the place all the time—they came back in and said, 'That was a great flight. All the flight attendants were good. They weren't yelling and screaming about their working conditions.' Everyone was saying this group [union negotiators] must be just representing themselves. . . ."[15]

Learning of the company's plan, Mary Lyn Moseley, master executive council chairperson for UAL flight attendants, protested to the president of UAL on March 10, 1975, by mailgram and again on March 12, 1975. On March 17, 1975, Moseley went to New York to meet with the union attorneys regarding the information centers. Arriving at La Guardia Airport, Moseley decided to stop at the information center before going to the lawyers' offices. The supervisor did not know Moseley or that she held the highest union position for flight attendants on United. After her information session with the company representative, Moseley went directly to the union law offices to fill out her affidavit to obtain injunctive relief against UAL: "The management representative with whom I met pursuant to United's program told me that no negotiations had even taken place. As a participant in the current negotiations, I know for a fact that the parties have engaged in 44 days of direct negotiations, and further met on 16 occasions in mediation. . . . I have received reports of similar conferences at United bases throughout the country. . . ."[16]

On the same day the judge for the eastern district of New York issued a temporary restraining order against United Airlines, directing UAL to cease direct negotiations with the employees and to negotiate only with their certified bargaining representative.[17] United quietly and quickly removed the informational centers from their properties.

The negotiating team continued in mediation but was unable to obtain a release from the National Mediation Board. "We had tried to train the company; many never did get the 'big picture,'" Rohde recalled, "and we had gone to the membership. What surprised us most of all was that the National Mediation Board had to be trained. . . ."[18]

One person who did not need enlightening about the determination of the stewardesses to be taken seriously was ALPA president J. J. O'Donnell. When O'Donnell was contacted by the National Mediation Board regarding an issue that the AFA negotiating team felt should have been addressed to them, he agreed with the women. O'Donnell had been through the reorganization of the S & S Division that yielded the Association of Flight Attendants, and he apparently needed no convincing that stewardesses should be taken seriously.

During the long negotiations the more than 300 issues of the union had been whittled down to 167, and in a mediated session held in San Diego in September 1975, the number was further reduced to approximately 100 unresolved items. But important issues were still on the table, and there were new developments on both negotiating teams. In November 1975, Diane Robertson, long-time union worker, had joined the negotiation committee after she was elected the new master executive council chairperson; Duane Buckmaster, the new senior vice president of personnel and industrial relations for UAL had joined the company team. "Mr. Buckmaster seemed to be the first person in that position to recognize the disparity between pilots and the flight attendants regarding such items as single rooms, cross-town travel, and duty time extensions," Robertson stated.[19] Negotiator Rohde concurred: "It is not to say that Chuck Thomson did not get the 'big picture.' He did. But it was not until November of 1975 that we got the first indication that the company hierarchy was listening to their own negotiators."[20]

The bargaining environment was further and perhaps drastically altered in December 1975 when the International Association of Machinists and Aerospace Workers (IAMAW) struck United Airlines. The women negotiators had been annoyed with the National Mediation Board for not releasing them from mediation, and now they were angry that the mechanics' union had obtained a release even though that group had been in negotiations for only ninety days; the flight attendants had been in negotiations for over eighteen months. Although accused of having a laundry list of unresolved items, the flight attendant union representatives knew that strikes were sometimes called over one unresolved item.

The union negotiators made valuable use of the strike time. Sue Bianchi, based in Washington, D.C., mobilized a campaign against the National Mediation Board. Working with several AFA women, including Iris Peterson, who had been the first flight attendant union lobbyist in Washington, D.C., the women covered the Hill. The negotiating committee had previously discussed the benefits of a "political blitz" on Capitol Hill if the National Mediation Board held the flight attendants in prolonged mediation.[21] According to Duane Buckmaster, company officials knew that some politicians had been contacted and had asked the National Mediation Board procedural questions about releasing the flight attendants.

Some main issues still in dispute revolved around certain rules beneficial to pilots that had nothing to do with flying the airplane, such as ground compensation for travel from one airport to another within the same general area. AFA was making issues out of these points and sought to bring a better balance in the working conditions among members of the flight crews, especially as they pertained to ground pay, holding time, cross-town travel, and prolonged duty periods.

"I represent the company—it is not my job to 'give away,'" Buckmaster said. "But at the same time I believed that it was my responsibility to both the company and the union to take a dispassionate look at these problems." He had lengthy discussion with the top management in UAL and mentioned there that the attitudes of the flight attendant union about the job and the desire for esteem had clearly changed.[22]

The company was ready to make some concessions in negotiations. Factors coinciding with the breakdown in negotiations worked to the union's advantage. Economist and labor arbitrator Mark L. Kahn observed that, "United had lost its strike-free image and feared that a thirty-day status quo period might cause another massive loss of traffic by apprehensive customers. It was in this context that United's flight attendant negotiations were rapidly consummated, still under mediation, and full agreement was reached on January 30, 1976, on terms more advantageous to the AFA than the company had previously been willing to grant. . . ."[23]

The 1974–77 contractual agreement between the Association of Flight Attendants and United Airlines was quickly dubbed the Green Book and was ratified by 85.9 percent of the membership.[24] Base pay brackets in the 1946 agreement raised the beginning salary from $120 a month for unlimited hourly flying to $155 a month for flight hours restricted to eighty-five a month. The agreement raised the base pay from $500 for beginning salary to $655 for the first six months earned for sixty-five hours of flying or guaranteed in a reserve status. Flight attendants could still opt to fly eighty-five hours a month or be scheduled to fly up to eighty hours a month. Measured in monetary terms as being worth approximately $61 million, the Green Book brought additional changes to many of the rank and file: retirement plans and benefits, single hotel rooms at rest points, and full retroactive pay during the protracted negotiations were among more than fifty significant improvements that had been negotiated.[25]

One of the most emotionally charged items in the Green Book was the single hotel room at layover points. The best that Ada Brown had been able to negotiate in 1946 was that no more than two stewardesses would be assigned to one room and that each would have a separate bed. For the next three decades flying partners shared hotel rooms. (When UAL commenced hiring male flight attendants for domestic operations in 1972, it was rare that more than one male was on a crew, so the steward was usually guaranteed his own room.) One item that the 1976 agreement did not achieve was additional holiday pay for being required to work on national holidays.

The future financial health of the national association of AFA had been enhanced, but progress of a more important sort was noted by Robertson: "The accomplishment of the 1974 negotiations committee was phenomenal in the way that it educated its membership. It finally gave the membership an awareness and raised the consciousness of the membership, which was needed before we could be a force to be reckoned with seriously by management. . . ."[26]

The signing of the Green Book also marked an unnoticed anniversary. It had been just thirty years since the tiny ALSA, under the leadership of Ada J. Brown, had coped with protracted and difficult negotiations for the first contractual agreement between stewardesses and a corporation in the United States, which was concluded on April 25, 1946. In 1976 a few of Ada J. Brown's early members and officers were still senior flight attendants for United Airlines.

The negotiations of 1946 and 1976 have much more in common than would be obvious by reading the contracts. In the areas of unofficial recognition and esteem for the occupation, it appears that the clock had stopped. The sexual exploitation evident in the marketing tactics of the airlines had crept into the processes at the negotiating table. For Ada Brown in 1946, it had been extremely important that the union receive a formal recognition, otherwise negotiations would be of little value. In 1976, her successor union was struggling for the degree of recognition essential to implement negotiated provisions.

Every word in the first contract was breaking barriers and new ground. Without the benefits of a revival of feminism, Ada Brown was able to lay the basic framework for a union for flight attendants. She and the first negotiating team had dealt with wage increases, a reduction in "hard time" or flight hours, and they had managed to negotiate grievance procedures and access to company-held information pertaining to individual attendants. Finally, the first union had achieved voluntary recognition.

For the first time since 1946, the union changed the format of Ada Brown's contractual agreement booklet. The practice of putting a vertical line in the margin of the agreement to denote new language began, and the 1976 contract is lined throughout its 232 pages with changes.

One significant change prohibits discrimination on account of sex and further prevents abridgments of equality because of "such individual's race, color, religion, national origin, age or marital status."[27]

During the first half of the 1970s, AFA's national officers were having problems keeping some factions of the union together. It is improbable that any president could have persuaded the unhappy groups to retain alliance with AFA. The various airlines with flight attendants under AFA had different levels of labor relations experience, and flight attendants were quick to blame the union for failure to achieve satisfactory contractual agreements. Some local leaders were conditioned to deal with the effects rather than with the causes of failures.

When National Airlines flight attendants withdrew their services on September 1, 1975, in a strike that grounded the airline for four and a half months, the AFA members failed, by a narrow margin, to pass a strike assessment ballot. By voting against the economic and psychological assistance that could have been provided, the AFA membership exposed their lack of coalition. Even though a hardship fund was set up by the AFA executive board for support of the National flight attendant group, bitterness and frustration resulted. National flight attendants voted to leave AFA in favor of the Transport Workers Union.

Northwest Airlines flight attendants, dissatisfied with their new AFA contract, geared up for yet another representational election in 1976. Disruptions by strikes and labor strife on Northwest were so common that some employees claimed they bid their annual vacations to coincide with possible strike dates. By March 1976, Northwest flight attendants voted to affiliate with the International Brotherhood of Teamsters. (At that time Teamster raids also posed a threat to AFA's retention of the approximately twelve hundred Western Airlines flight attendants.)

AFA also encountered problems with retaining the Continental Airlines flight attendants. The Continental attendants had been under the leadership of Darenda Hardy since the early 1970s. In the mid-1970s she was the master executive council chairperson for the Continental flight attendants in AFA. During the reorganization that transformed the S & S Division to AFA, her position had, at times, been less compromising than for some of the other leaders. At one point she recommended giving the pilots an ultimatum to either allow the S & S

Division voting rights within ALPA and all other benefits of the pilot union or to see the stewardesses leave.[28] While she had some supporters, a large number on the board of directors did not share her either-or position on that issue.

A member of the negotiating team for the Continental flight attendants in 1976, Hardy believed that during a crucial point of the negotiations, AFA removed its staff negotiator, who had been provided by the national office. This was done without consulting the Continental negotiating committee, according to Hardy, and she later wrote that this had a serious impact on negotiations. The team insisted that the action be rescinded, but to no avail. Recalling the incident, Hardy later added that this disastrous intervention was "the last straw in a long series of disputes over such matters with AFA."[29] Two months later there was an election, and the Union of Flight Attendants, Local No. 1, was certified as the bargaining agent for Continental flight attendants on November 15, 1976. The new union won by a three-to-one margin. By 1977, Wien Air Alaska flight attendants also voted to leave AFA; that group, however, joined the Teamsters for representation.

Part of AFA's vulnerability lay in its democratic structure. The AFA board of directors, composed of all local council chairpersons, is the highest governing body for the union and creates policy for the union. Its liberal policies make it difficult to create trusteeships within dissident ranks. Before any action can be taken, a twenty-day written notice must be given to the alleged violators or violator. This generous schedule allows a dissident group or leader to mobilize for action against AFA.

Having lost Wien, Northwest, National, and Continental, AFA's membership still stood at around twenty thousand. But partially due to the costs of trying to retain Continental, Northwest, National, and Wien, AFA was beset by financial difficulties. The union could either emerge as a strong force, or it could collapse.

During this upheaval a growing internal cohesiveness was exhibited by the United flight attendants. The UAL membership, AFA's largest group with approximately eight thousand members worked for more than a year under an unamended contract renewable in October 1974. The UAL flight attendants adopted the slogan "It's our turn," and continued to support their negotiators.

Almost as soon as the 1974 agreement was signed into effect in 1976, it was time to commence renegotiating for the 1978 agreement. The same union negotiating team remained intact, except for one replacement, and the company team retained at least one negotiator from the Green Book. Both the company and the union were optimistic. A new level of awareness was working in their favor, and they had negotiated an expedited process for arriving at the 1978 agreement.

During the latter months of 1977, the union and the company were in effective and productive negotiations. The union proposal was aimed at improving retirement and savings provisions, salary increases, working conditions for reserves, and the holiday pay compensation, among other items. The company was interested in the usual increase of utilization of the flight attendants. Signing an agreement on time, the company and the union representatives were pleased with the contract. Union negotiator Sue Bianchi said, "We all knew it was a good contract within the industry and from a historical perspective."

Something went awry. The membership voted the 1978 agreement down: 2,613 against and 2,011 for, out of the 7,127 eligible to vote. The union and the company officials were stunned. The union team considered resigning, then realized that it would be beneficial to find out what the members did not like about the agreement and renegotiate.

It was up to the union negotiators to conduct road shows and to formulate new proposals to correspond to the members' demands. During the road shows several union weaknesses became apparent. Some members had sent in their ballots before attending meetings for explanations, and many had not gone to earlier informational sessions regarding the proposed contract. This was most likely because membership ratification was relatively new for United flight attendants. Before the 1970s the master executive council ratified the contracts. The AFA constitution and bylaws leave the ratification question up to the various carriers' master executive councils, composed of the local chairpersons. Also, the expedited negotiation process had been in sharp contrast to the long, agonizing months of confrontation over the previous Green Book contract, during which the members had had an opportunity to become involved in the issues to a greater degree.

The dissatisfactions with the 1978 tentative agreement seemed to center around the new provisions for reserve status and for implementation dates for new compensation and rules that would last throughout the two-year life of the contract. The implementation dates for various provisions in previous contracts had not been unusual (e.g., pay raises are scheduled for the duration of many agreements). For the flight attendants, some who had only recently taken an interest in union activities, the kick-in dates were unacceptable. They did not want to wait until the next year for relief.[30]

Sue Bianchi, a negotiator for the union, was somewhat uncomfortable with the tentative agreement. While she thought it was a good agreement, she also knew that some things were left out, and she was not sure that the membership would accept anything less than everything. Local council officer Kathy Hutchens candidly told members at a council meeting that "not every contract can be a "green book" and flight attendants have to understand that."[31]

According to company negotiator Chuck Thomson, the 1978 negotiations were transitional. The union and the company were involved in problem solving. When the membership turned down the tentative 1978 contractual agreement, both the company and the union negotiators realized that they were ahead of the membership.[32]

After touring the system the union negotiators decided to negotiate for provisions that flight attendants had voiced a need for, down to the wire. The company was uncomfortable with the crisis situation of negotiating to the strike deadline. Business could be lost due to the threat of an impending strike. The union membership would have to be made aware that if they voted against the next tentative agreement they, in effect, would be taking the responsibility, that they must be willing to strike and to walk the picket lines when they vote against a negotiated tentative contract. Preparations for a strike were set into motion. The union officers began the time-consuming and costly processes of setting up picketing schedules and other strike measures.

At the negotiating table, the procedures for the reserve status provisions were renegotiated, and and changes were made. Other items were left open and were actively negotiated within a few minutes of the strike deadline. At that point the negotiators signed a second tentative agreement and sent it out to the membership on December 22, 1977. The members ratitifed it: 4,937 for, 914 against, and 103 void ballots. Eighty-four percent of the 7,127 eligible members had voted.[33]

The rejection of the 1978 Blue Book signaled the union and the company negotiators that traditional methods needed to be changed and some new solutions should be applied. Additionally, the problem of the management personnel responsible for and to the flight attendants needed attention.

Independently, Susan Rohde, as master executive chairperson for the UAL flight attendants, and Chuck Thomson, as director of industrial relations, inflight services, began to explore various ideas for a quality of work life program to solve some of the division's problems. After Rohde and Thomson had attended a two-week course at UCLA, the first inflight quality of work life (QWL) program for flight attendants commenced very cautiously. Dividing up into committees, each group would be assigned one of four subjects to research and report on to the body. Defined problems for committee work included philosophy, contract administration, grievances, and pilferage (which the company managers considered a problem at the time).

While the quality of work life teams were careful to point out that no negotiable items would be discussed in such sessions, some residual effects were occurring. When the company and the union met in early 1980 for the negotiations for the 1980 contractual agreement, they had been in session for two weeks when the company announced it planned to furlough around five hundred flight attendants and asked for any alternatives from the negotiating team. The union came up with a partnership time-off plan whereby the flight attendants could double up and work the same schedule (Independent Union of Flight Attendants, representing Pan American's flight attendants, had devised a similar plan).[34] In effect, two flight attendants would work as one. They could divide their pay and flight time according to their desires.[35] From the company's viewpoint the partnership program was acceptable because it saved money while keeping a full work force on deck. For the union, the plan saved jobs. Under those conditions, it was implemented; either the company or the union could terminate the program.

The 1980–82 contract, United flight attendants' nineteenth bargaining agreement, won a 24.3 percent increase in pay compounded over a twenty-four-month period. Starting with no extra compensation for holiday pay, the union was able to negotiate pay for ten holidays with a formula that rendered close to double pay for flight attendants who would be in the workplace away from their families during holidays. Guaranteed personal time off ensured the flight attendants that they could ask for at least three work days yearly for personal reasons, and no reason would have to be given to the company. According to seniority, a percentage of flight attendants at each domicile could have the personal time off every day of the year.

A flight attendant in his or her tenth year of flying UAL's domestic routes could earn a maximum of about $24,000.[36] Full pay and flight time credit for all deadhead hours were negotiated, a provision that had been developing at various levels of relief since the late 1940s. During the early 1950s flight attendants were neither paid nor credited any hours for deadhead. Consequently, they were indiscriminately dispatched all over the system in a deadhead status. With no pay liabilities, the company did not have to concern itself with inconveniences to the flight attendants.[37] Long-term disability insurance equal to 50 percent of monthly salary was also negotiated; the plan was optional and the cost was $0.19 per $100 of salary per month. The Federal Aviation Regulations for crew complement were written into the contractual agreement for scheduling purposes. The crew complement issue was timely: before the 1980 contract was amendable, the FAA proposed a cutback in crew complement requirements. The contract for 1980–82 was ratified by 94 percent of the 70 percent eligible membership who voted.[38]

In their shortest negotiations since 1945, the union and UAL agreed on a side letter to the 1980–82 contract that extended the contract for one year and granted a 10 percent increase in pay and per diem expense. The membership ratified the side letter.

In 1981, the Association of Flight Attendants, an autonomous union, affiliated with the Air Line Pilots Association, represented around half the unionized flight attendants in the United States or 22,115. Administered and run by the women themselves, AFA was the largest of the few predominantly female unions in the country. As such, it was unique.

The other six flight attendant unions in the United States were factionalized and had a combined membership of almost the same size as AFA. Their collective bargaining rights were held by various independents, the Teamsters, and the Transport Workers Union.

The largest number with AFA and the biggest single group of flight attendants employed by an airline was the United membership, who numbered 9,358. The other airlines represented by AFA in order of size were as follows: Braniff, 2,959 (declared bankruptcy in 1982); Western, 2,194; USAir, 1,484; Republic, 1,446; Republic West, 901; Frontier, 778; Trans America, 667; Piedmont, 628; Ozark, 525; Texas International, 466; Overseas National (undergoing corporate reorganization), 250; Alaska, 226; Hawaiian, 221; Aloha Airlines, 126; Airlift International, 43; Air New England, 23 (dissolved in 1981); and New York Airways (dissolved in 1980), 15.[39]

The Transport Workers Union represented the following groups: AirCal, 256; Eastern Airlines, 6,600; and Southwest Airlines, 303. The International Brotherhood of Teamsters held Capitol, approximately 400; Flying Tiger, approximately 400 (in 1982 these attendants joined AFA); Northwest, approximately 2,600; World, approximately 900; Pacific Southwest, approximately 750; and Wien Air Alaska, approximately 140.[40]

Four independent unions formed in the 1970s, and their numbers total about nineteen thousand members. Pan American World Airways flight attendants are represented by the Independent Union of Flight Attendants (IUFA), largest of the independents. National Airlines, which merged with Pan American in 1979, increased IUFA's numbers from a few more than five thousand to around seven thousand.[41] (IUFA secured bargaining rights for the ex-National flight attendants with almost no challenge, partially because National members had undergone bitter fights with both ALPA and TWU within the previous decade.)

Trans World Airlines flight attendants, numbering around 6,000 are represented by the Independent Federation of Flight Attendants (IFFA). The Association of Professional Flight Attendants (APFA) represents around 6,100 for American Airlines; and, the smallest independent group is the Union of Flight Attendants (UFA), Local No. 1, representing 1,869 Continental Airlines cabin attendants.[42]

At the end of the 1970s, the Transport Workers Union, AFA's largest rival union competitor, underwent enormous upheaval. Charging male domination, more than sixteen thousand flight attendants voted to disaffilate with TWU. Within one year, flight attendants on Trans World Airlines, Pan American Airways, and American Airlines disaffiliated and formed their own independent and unaffiliated unions.

AFA did not gain these dissident groups. Believing that AFA was still under the thumb of the Air Line Pilots Association, some of the newly formed unions wanted no part of affiliation with other "male dominated" members of AFL-CIO.[43]

The stewardesses, who numbered four out of five of the flight attendant membership of TWU, were clearly retrenching for independence. The new names of the independent unions also reveal the flight attendants' search for identity. There was every indication that the flight attendants, who were closely linked with other airline workers within TWU, especially in the case of Pan American attendants, wanted to break from the other work groups and to present themselves as a flight attendant union. American Airlines flight attendants went so far as to call their new independent union the Association of Professional Flight Attendants.

Few, if any, of the leaders of dissident TWU flight attendants were willing to accept an affiliation with the AFA. The legacy of the close relationship of AFA to the pilot union was a negative factor for the independent leaders. During the late 1970s a back debt owed to the pilot union by the Association of Flight Attendants was also cited by leaders of the new independent unions as a drawback to joining AFA.[44]

When asked about the unrest in the rival flight attendant unions, Pat Robertson, former AFA president, stated, "We know the source of unrest. It was out of that very unrest that AFA emerged as a viable force to deal with the management and with the regulators in our industry."[45] She later added, "Eventually they'll all come back together; it's tough out there by yourself."[46] AFA itself had changed since the upheaval of the 1970s. Constitutional changes have been made; by 1980, the treasury showed its first surplus in history;[47] and the bargaining rights had been officially gained by the Association of Flight Attendants for all member carriers. Some of these changes were accompanied by conflict, but the union continued to run relatively smoothly. Most of AFA's officers agreed that one of the most significant changes in the union was the requirement for the board of directors to meet each year, which enables the directors to maintain closer contact with the executive board as well as the national officers.[48]

The executive board is composed of the master executive council chairpersons from each carrier. That officer is the highest ranking union representative on each carrier and acts in an ex-officio role at the board of directors meetings. Policy for the executive board is set by the board of directors and has specific restrictions in that it cannot change the constitution and bylaws, change the dues structure, or levy assessments. The duties of the executive board are to carry out the provisions of the constitution as mandated by the board of directors. The executive board wields considerable clout in dictating both to the national officers and to the local council officers whom they lead, the general direction of the union.

Pat Robertson, AFA's president in 1979, encountered serious difficulties in her administration. The executive board had put her on warning that the hired staff of AFA had to be reevaluated and some should be replaced. In 1978, the board of directors had asked for the firing of one staff member who had been heavily involved in negotiations for the various carriers.

The internal politics of the union were changing. Some wanted the executive board to be able to exercise a roll-call vote, if it desired. It had been operating under a one-person, one-vote concept. There was a fear by some of the smaller carriers that the large carriers would dominate the executive board. Robertson opposed this obviously radical change.

Meanwhile, the staff at the AFA national office had formed their own internal union. Quick to point out that they were not against unionization of the staff, some officers wondered if the mobilization was yet another dissatisfaction with Robertson's administration. As it turned out, the staff was quite loyal to Robertson and many threatened to resign if Robertson was recalled.[49] Confidence of the majority of the elected officers in Robertson's administration was waning. At the 1979 board of directors meeting, thirty-eight councils, representing 11,586 active members, voted to recall Pat Robertson as president of AFA. The board officially listed the reasons for the recall as disregard for directives issued by the board on issues involving the dismissal of the coordinator of contract administration and on the issue of organizing at American Airlines; internal administrative staff problems that resulted in disruption of services in the field; internal administrative problems that resulted in critical staff attrition problems at the national office; responsibility for an inaccurate projected dues income shown for the 1979 budget, which resulted in a totally erroneous budget projection; inability to control the increasing financial problems facing the union; and a disregard for effectively dealing with the problems as stated in the 1978 board of directors transcript letters from the local executive council chairpersons and the master executive council chairpersons.[50]

Holding elections to select the new national president and vice president of AFA, the board chose Linda Puchala, the master executive council chairperson from Republic Airlines, as president and Susan Bianchi Sand, a flight attendant with United Airlines and a local council chairperson for AFA, as vice president. Pamela Casey, a flight attendant from Alaska Airlines, remained the secretary-treasurer. All three women had union experience.

Puchala had one opponent in the 1979 elections. A male flight attendant from Western Airlines ran as a serious candidate, but lost by a thirteen-to-one margin. Puchala was overwhelmingly elected by the board of directors. The union representing predominantly female flight attendants had changed much since the days in 1953 when a male flight attendant had gained support to lead their union partially because he was a man. While it is not unusual for male flight attendants to be elected as officers within AFA, sex did not seem to determine the board's support.

Taking over the presidency, Linda Puchala began the difficult task of leading a large union with diverse constituencies. By 1980, her influence was evident in the union's ability to cope with a rapidly changing industry. At the 1980 board of directors meeting, the officers of AFA faced the challenges of the Airline Deregulation Act of 1978 and the strain of rising fuel prices on the airline industry. Bankruptcies, mergers, acquisitions, furloughs, and domicile closures were the early effects of deregulation. Flight attendants continued to be used as lures especially among the new small airlines in heavy promotion campaigns to capture more business in the intensely competitive environment. Some airline officials stressed that flight attendants' attitudes could make the difference in passenger acceptance of curtailing or eliminating inflight amenities, including food services.

Discount fares, increased seating capacities on airplanes, and corporate restructuring greatly affected the workplace. Flight attendants looked to their unions to provide guidance with furloughs, recalls, expanding routes, contracting routes, opening new domiciles, closing domiciles, and management changes. Union officers had increasing responsibilities to safeguard the well-being of their members as new airlines were created and old airlines became parent companies to new ones. Perhaps more than ever before, the members of the flight attendant unions needed their union representatives to assist them with these transitions.

The members of AFA varied widely in their awareness of unionism and democracy and in their expectations of their union officers. But Kathy Hutchens, who represented more than fourteen hundred UAL flight attendants at the San Francisco base, asserted that "we cannot coddle the members; our structure demands a knowledge of the union. Fortunately, many of them now know what they have."[52]

Notes

Unless otherwise specified, the source for the correspondence and other unpublished documents cited in these notes is the files of the Association of Flight Attendants, Washington, D.C.

Chapter 1

1. Alexander C. Morton, *The 1979–80 Guide to Stewardess and Steward Careers*, ed. Linda Hamblin and Mary Thompson (New York: Arco, 1979), p. 10.

2. Interview with Barbara Noyer, Burlingame, California, December 12, 1978.

3. *United Mainliner* 24, 5 (May 1980): 52.

4. *Boeing System Stewardess Manual*, Boeing inhouse publication, San Francisco, January 1931, p. 5.

5. Joseph D. Alter and Stanley R. Mohler, "Preventive Medicine Aspects and Health Promotion Programs for Flight Attendants," paper presented at the International Aviation and Space Medicine Conference, Manila, Philippines, October 8–12, 1981, p. 2.

6. Leslie Taylor, ed., *Air Transport, 1981: The Annual Report of the U.S. Scheduled Airline Industry* (Washington, D.C.: Air Transport Association, 1980), p. 11; and J. Kastner, "Joan Waltermire: Air Stewardess," *Life*, April 28, 1941.

7. Data supplied from April 1, 1981, inventory by Jean Widenmyer, director of accounting and membership, and Helen Schalet, research analyst, Association of Flight Attendants, April 7, 1981. Due to airline mergers, carrier representation figures change frequently.

8. Carl Solberg, *Conquest of the Skies: A History of Commercial Aviation in America* (Boston: Little, Brown Co., 1979), p. 23; and George E. Hopkins, *The Airline Pilots: A Study in Elite Unionization* (Cambridge, Mass.: Harvard University Press, 1971), pp. 11–16, p. 34.

9. Ibid., p. 63.

10. Ibid., p. 139.

11. Henry Ladd Smith, *Airways* (New York: Russell & Russell, 1965), pp. 158, 160, 377–79.

12. Solberg, *Conquest of the Skies*, pp. 110–13.

13. Frank J. Taylor, *"Pat" Patterson* (Menlo Park: Lane Magazine and Book Co., 1967), pp. 34–36.

14. Paula Kane, *Sex Objects in the Sky* (Chicago: Follett Publishing Co., 1975), p. 97.

15. Interview with Mary O'Connor, Chicago, Illinois, February 13, 1979.

16. Frank J. Taylor, *High Horizons* (New York: McGraw-Hill Co., 1951), pp. 69–71.

17. Taylor, *"Pat" Patterson*, p. 35.

18. Telephone interview with George E. Hopkins, May 31, 1981; telephone interview with Earl Marquis, researcher, Air Line Pilots Association, Washington, D.C., March 31, 1982, citing ALPA minutes from 1935 and 1936; and Valorie Moolman, *Women Aloft* (Alexandria, Va.: Time-Life Books, 1981), p. 13.

19. Ellen Church, introduction to *Skygirl*, by Mary F. Murray (New York: Duell, Sloan, and Pearce, 1951), p. 13.

20. Taylor, *"Pat" Patterson*, pp. 34–35.

21. Ibid., p. 36.

22. Kane, *Sex Objects in the Sky*, pp. 98–99. Even before the mail contracts had been canceled in 1934, most airlines were warming up to the idea of women working on airplanes. But, as president of Eastern Airlines, Rickenbacker let all flight attendants go in 1934 and then hired only men for the job until World War II diminished the supply of men for home front jobs. Pan American also retained only men as cabin attendants until 1944 and later claimed that Pan Am's international route structure demanded skills more in tune with male cabin attendants.

23. S. S. Peoria, "History of the Air Line Stewardess," *Service Aloft* 1, 3 (December 1946): 3.

24. Taylor, *"Pat" Patterson*, p. 36.

25. Ibid. See also Taylor, *High Horizons*, p. 71.

26. "Stewardess Recruits Much in Demand," *Air Travel*, May 1965, p. 1.

27. Kenneth Hudson, *Air Travel: A Social History* (Totowa, N.J.: Rowman and Littlefield, 1972), p. 43.

28. "In Flight with the Early Birds," *California Living Magazine*, in *San Francisco Sunday Examiner and Chronicle*, May 4, 1980, pp. 70–73.

29. "Stewardess 1930 Style," *New York Times*, May 15, 1970.

30. Ellen Church, introduction to *Skygirl*, by Mary F. Murray, p. 13.

31. Hopkins, *The Airline Pilots*, pp. 5–18.

32. Mary O'Connor, *Flying Mary O'Connor* (New York: Rand McNally and Co., 1961), p. 14.

33. Ibid., p. 25.

34. "Stewardess 1930 Style."

35. *Boeing Stewardess Manual*, January 1931, p. 19.

36. Solberg, *Conquest of the Skies*, p. 215.

37. George E. Hopkins, "Flying the Line," *Air Line Pilot* 50, 5 (May 1981): 25.

38. Solberg, *Conquest of the Skies*, pp. 138–40, 143–48; and Norman E. Borden, Jr., *Air Mail Emergency 1934* (Freeport, Maine: Bond Wheelwright Co., 1968).

39. Mark Kahn, "Airlines," in *Collective Bargaining: Contemporary American Experience*, edited by Gerald G. Somers (Madison, Wis.: Industrial Relations Research Association, 1980), p. 318.

40. Ibid., pp. 315–72.

41. Christopher Chant, *Aviation: An Illustrated History* (London: Orbis Publishing Co., 1978), pp. 176–77.

42. "Air Hostess Must Meet High Ideals," *Sunday Star* (Washington, D.C.), April 3, 1938.

43. Solberg, *Conquest of the Skies*, p. 33.

44. Interviews with Edith Lauterbach, San Francisco, California, March 4, 1976, and May 15, 1981.

45. Kahn, "Airlines," p. 324.

46. Victor J. Herbert, acting president, Air Line Stewards and Stewardesses Association, International, to John M. Chamberlain, director, Bureau of Safety Regulation, Civil Aeronautics Board, March 27, 1951.

47. Interview with Victor J. Herbert, president, Air Line Employees Association, Chicago, Illinois, March 20, 1981.

48. "Air Hostess Must Meet High Ideals."

49. *Sprogis v. United Airlines, Inc.*, 308 F. Supp. 959 (1970), aff'd F2d 1194, *cert. denied*, 404 U.S. 991.

50. Interview with Ed Westerfelt, United Airlines industrial relations administrator, Chicago, Illinois, March 19, 1981.

51. Passenger conversation with author in 1966.

52. Westerfelt interview.

53. United Airlines Stewardesses' System Board of Adjustment, Board No. 66-1, referee Mark L. Kahn, April 21, 1967, p. 14.

54. Interview with John R. Hill, retired United Airlines legal counsel, Santa Barbara, California, March 7, 1981.

55. O'Connor interview.

56. O'Connor, *Flying Mary O'Connor*, pp. 59–60.

57. O'Connor interview.

58. John M. Baitsell, *Airline Industrial Relations: Pilots and Flight Engineers* (Cambridge, Mass.: Harvard University Press, 1966), p. 29; and Hopkins, *The Airline Pilots*, pp. 1–18.

59. "Greetings on Our 15th Anniversary . . . Your United Stewardesses," United Airlines inhouse publication, undated.

60. *How to Become a Mainliner Stewardess*, United Airlines inhouse publications, undated.

Chapter 2

1. George E. Hopkins, *The Airline Pilots: A Study in Elite Unionization* (Cambridge, Mass.: Harvard University Press, 1971), p. 189; and CAA, *Statistical Handbook of Civil Aviation*, 1944, p. 33, and *FAA Statistical Handbook of Aviation*, 1959, pp. 28, 75–76, 91, 93, cited in John M. Baitsell, *Airline Industrial Relations: Pilots and Flight Engineers* (Cambridge, Mass.: Harvard University Press, 1966).

2. Charles M. Rehmus, "Evolution of Legislation Affecting Collective Bargaining in the Railroad and Airline Industries," in *The Railway Labor Act at Fifty* (Washington, D.C.: U.S. Government Printing Office, 1977), pp. 7–10.

3. Joseph Krislov, "Mediation under the Railway Labor Act: A Process in Search of a Name," *Labor Law Journal* 1, 5 (May 1976): 310–15.

4. 45 U.S.C. §§ 151–188 (1976).

5. Hopkins, *The Airline Pilots*, pp. 132–41, 178–81; and Mark Kahn, "Airlines," in *Collective Bargaining: Contemporary American Experience*, edited by Gerald G. Somers (Madison, Wis.: Industrial Relations Research Association), pp. 340–42.

6. Baitsell, *Airline Industrial Relations*, p. 34; and Kahn, "Airlines," p. 349.

7. Interview with John R. Hill, Santa Barbara, California, March 7, 1981.

8. Ibid.

9. Interviews with Edith Lauterbach, San Francisco, California, March 4, 1976, and May 15, 1981.

10. Figures from J. Kastner, "Joan Waltermire: Air Stewardess," *Life*, April 28, 1941, pp. 102–12; *Air Transport: The Annual Report of the U.S. Scheduled Airline Industry* [titled *Facts and Figures* before 1970] (Washington, D.C.: Air Transport Association, various editions through 1978), cited by Mark Kahn, "Airlines," in *Collective Bargaining: Contemporary American Experience*, edited by Gerald G. Somers (Madison, Wis.: Industrial Relations Research Association, 1980), p. 333, table 6; Leslie Taylor, ed., *Air Transport 1980: The Annual Report of the U.S. Scheduled Airline Industry* (Washington, D.C.: Air Transport Association, 1980); and Form 10-K: Annual Report Pursuant to Section 13 or 15(d) of the Securities Exchange Act of 1934, UAL, Inc., for the fiscal year ended December 31, 1980, p. 10.

11. Interviews with Ada J. Brown Greenfield, St. Helena, California, March 12, 1976; Aptos, California, March 7, 1979; and Los Angeles, California, November 1 and 2, 1980.

12. Hill interview.

13. Telephone interview with Charles F. McErlean, retired United Airlines vice president, March 19, 1981.

14. Interview with Sally Thometz Hall, Los Angeles, California, November 2, 1980.

15. Interviews with Kathy Hutchens, San Francisco, California, April 3, 1979, September 5, 1980, and March 2 and 24, 1981.

16. Ada J. Brown to David L. Behncke, July 27, 1945; and Brown Greenfield interviews.

666

666

666

666

Notes

17. Brown to Behncke, July 27, 1945.

18. Constitution and Bylaws of the Air Line Stewardesses Association. Adapted from the Constitution and Bylaws of the Air Line Pilots Association, International, adopted September 1945 (cover page of constitution and bylaws of ALSA as revised January 1947). The organization date of the Air Line Stewardesses Association was June 7, 1945, and the union was officially established and recognized August 22, 1945.

19. Committee Resolution—Final Form, ALPA 1944 Convention, File No. 38: Relation between ALPA and other Employee-Representing Groups in the Air Industry.

20. Interview with Victor J. Herbert, president, Air Line Employees Association, Chicago, Illinois, March 20, 1981.

21. Ibid.; and Victor J. Herbert to David L. Behncke, Outline of Education and Organization Department, February 10, 1947.

22. Brown Greenfield interviews.

23. Brown to Behncke, July 27, 1945.

24. David L. Behncke to Ada Brown, August 22, 1945.

25. Brown Greenfield interviews.

26. Hopkins, The Airline Pilots, pp. 44–46.

27. Brown Greenfield interviews.

28. Adriano G. Delfino, Corporate and Legal History of United Air Lines, Inc. and Its Subsidiaries 1946–1955, vol. 2 (Elk Grove Township, Ill.: United Air Lines, 1965), pp. 1086–88.

29. Hill interview; McErlean interview; and Lauterbach interviews.

30. Lauterbach interviews.

31. Interview with Frances Hall Craft, Los Angeles, California, November 2, 1980.

32. Hill interview.

33. McErlean interview.

34. Lauterbach interviews.

35. Ibid.

36. Brown Greenfield interviews.

37. Hill interview.

38. Hall Craft interview.

39. Brown Greenfield interviews.

40. Hill interview.

41. Brown Greenfield interviews.

42. Delfino, History of United Air Lines, vol. 2, p. 1086, n. 100.

43. McErlean interview.

44. Franklin Gledhill, vice president, Pan American World Airways System, to R. F. Cole, secretary, National Mediation Board, November 9, 1945.

45. Agreement between United Air Lines, Inc. and Air Line Stewardesses in the Service of United Air Lines, Inc. as Represented by the Air Line Stewardesses Associa-

141

tion, January 1, 1946. Section 1, Recognition, p. 1, contains a preface confirming the date the agreement was made and entered into as April 25, 1946.

46. Hall Craft interview.

47. Sally Thometz Hall, speaking to the Association of Flight Attendants board of directors, Bonaventure Hotel, Los Angeles, California, November 2, 1980.

48. ALSA and UAL agreement January 1, 1946.

49. Lauterbach interviews.

50. Telephone interview with George E. Hopkins, May 31, 1981.

51. Delfino, *History of United Air Lines*, vol. 2, pp. 1086–87 n.

52. ALSA and UAL agreements, 1946, 1947, 1948, and 1949.

53. In the Matter of Air Lines [sic] Stewardesses Association and United Air Lines, Inc., decision of Stewardess System Board of Adjustment, 1949.

54. Hill interview.

55. ALSA grievance, 1949; and Hill interview.

56. "Honolulu Grievance Goes to the System Board of Adjustment," *WAL and UAL ALSA News* (Air Line Stewardesses Association), October 1948, p. 1.

57. Hill interview.

58. Lauterbach interviews.

59. Telephone interviews with Sheldon Kline, research director, National Mediation Board, October 23, 1980, and December 3, 1981; In the Matter of Representation of Employees of the Pan American Airways, Inc. Flight Stewards, Port Stewards, case no. R-1578, May 27, 1946; Maurice H. Forge, assistant secretary-treasurer, Transport Workers Union, to Robert F. Cole, secretary, National Mediation Board, April 10, 1946; Franklin Gledhill to Maurice Forge, May 23, 1946; and Franklin Gledhill to Douglas L. MacMahon, secretary-treasurer, Transport Workers Union of America, June 7, 1946.

60. Brown Greenfield interviews.

61. Interviews with Rowland K. Quinn, executive secretary, National Mediation Board, Washington, D.C., February 14, 1979, and March 16, 1981.

62. Ada J. Brown to all ALSA members, July 17, 1947, reprinted in Opening Remarks to the Sixth Biennial Convention of ALSSA, Int'l., by Rowland K. Quinn, Jr., president, April 11, 1961, pp. 1–4.

63. Brown Greenfield interviews.

64. David L. Behncke to all American Airlines pilots, May 15, 1947.

65. National Mediation Board certification of representation cases. See also "Flight Attendant Labor Organization," inhouse publication (Washington, D.C.: Transport Workers Union, un:dated); and "Merger Strengthens ALPA Stewards and Stewardess Affiliate," *ALPA News Bulletin* 1, 10, December 10, 1949.

66. Herbert interview.

67. Interviews with Irene Eastin, San Francisco, California, March 6 and 11, 1981.

68. National Mediation Board case no. R-2249 shows that of 556 eligible voters for UAL, 429 voted in the representational election. A card count verified a majority for

ALSSA. National Mediation Board case no. R-2250 shows Western had 81 eligible voters, of whom 62 voted.

69. Hill interview.

Chapter 3

1. Frank J. Taylor, *High Horizons* (New York: McGraw-Hill Co., 1951), p. 187.

2. Betty Friedan, *The Feminine Mystique* (New York: Dell Publishing Co., 1963), pp. 37, 47–48, 229.

3. William H. Chafe, *The American Woman: Her Changing Social, Economic, and Political Roles, 1920–1970* (London: Oxford University Press, 1972), p. 218.

4. "Supreme Court in Landmark Decision Dumps Brown Case," *Dispatcher* (published by the International Longshoremen's and Warehousemen's Union), June 11, 1965, p. 1.

5. Ada J. Brown to all ALSA members, July 17, 1947.

6. George Meany to Clarence N. Sayen, president, ALPA, March 14, 1957.

7. Minutes of AFL-CIO Meeting, Washington, D.C., June 11, 1961.

8. ALPA Constitution and Bylaws, as revised October 23, 1936, p. 12, cited in John M. Baitsell, *Airline Industrial Relations: Pilots and Flight Engineers* (Cambridge, Mass.: Harvard University Press, 1966), p. 211. In 1942 the racist clause in ALPA's constitution was changed.

9. Agreement between United Air Lines, Inc. and Air Line Stewardesses and Cabin Stewards in the Service of United Air Lines, Inc., as represented by Air Line Stewards and Stewardesses Association, International, 1950 Agreement, p. 52. See also Highlights of ALSSA-ALPA-TWU Activities as Taken from Available Records, undated; and History-Chronology, report of the ALPA S & S Study Committee, November 1972, Association of Flight Attendant files, Washington, D.C.

10. Interviews with Irene Eastin, San Francisco, California, March 6 and 11, 1981.

11. Proceedings of the First National Convention of ALSSA, 1951, pp. 12–13, cited by James Francis Hart, "The Effect of Union Shop on the Contracts of the Airline Stewards and Stewardesses Association" (master's thesis, De Paul University, 1969), p. 5; and *Service Aloft*, published by the ALSSA, Int'l., 5, 3 (April-May-June 1951): 1, 4.

12. *Service Aloft* 5, 3.

13. Transcript, David L. Behncke before the First Convention of the ALSSA, June 6, 1951.

14. *Service Aloft* 5, 3.

15. Telephone interviews with Mary Alice Koos Spencer on April 4, 1981, and May 5, 1981; and *Service Aloft* 1, 5.

16. *Service Aloft* 5, 3.

143

17. Koos Spencer interviews; and Hart, "Effect of Union Shop on Contracts," pp. 5, 12–13, 132.

18. Proceedings of Sixteenth Biennial Convention of ALPA, November 1960, pp. 1307, 2085; and Statement of Air Line Stewards and Stewardesses, Int'l, in Support of Its Application for a Charter of Affiliation from the AFL-CIO, undated (probably 1960).

19. Kathy Lukas, "The Evolution of the Flight Attendant Union Movement in the United States" (paper for the Department of Social Sciences, San Francisco State University, December 14, 1979), p. 12.

20. Interview with Victor J. Herbert, president, Air Line Employees Association, Chicago, Illinois, March 20, 1981.

21. Rowland K. Quinn, Jr., president, ALSSA, to AFL-CIO Executive Council, undated (probably 1960), with attached background report in petition for AFL-CIO charter.

22. Herbert interview; and Lukas, "Evolution of the Flight Attendant Union," p. 12.

23. Koos Spencer interviews.

24. *Dodd* v. *American Airlines*, EEOC Dec. (CCH) (1973) ¶6001.

25. Koos Spencer interviews.

26. Herbert interview.

27. Koos Spencer interviews.

28. Interviews with Rowland K. Quinn, executive secretary, National Mediation Board, Washington, D.C., February 14, 1979, and March 16, 1981.

29. Interviews with Edith Lauterbach, San Francisco, California, March 4, 1976, and May 15, 1981.

30. *Service Aloft* 7, 3 (April-September 1953).

31. Herbert interview.

32. Quinn interviews.

33. Proceedings of the Second National Convention of ALSSA, 1953, pp. 1–4, 26, cited by Hart, "Effect of Union Shop on Contracts," p. 6; and minutes of AFL-CIO meeting, January 11, 1961, p. 11.

34. Quinn interviews.

35. Interview with Paul Berthoud, director, industrial relations, ground employees, United Airlines, Chicago, Illinois, March 19, 1981.

36. Lauterbach interviews.

37. Proceedings of the Fourth National Convention of ALSSA, 1957, p. 17, cited by Hart, "Effect of Union Shop on Contracts," p. 7.

38. Rowland K. Quinn, Jr., president, Air Line Stewards and Stewardesses Association, Int'l, to C. N. Sayen, president, Air Line Pilots Association, May 2, 1957.

39. Proceedings of the Fourth National Convention, 1957, p. 17.

40. Baitsell, *Airline Industrial Relations*, pp. 187–225.

41. Berthoud interview.

42. Quinn interviews.

43. Ibid.

44. Lauterbach interviews.

45. Quinn interviews.

46. Lukas, "Evolution of Flight Attendant Union," p. 18.

47. Rowland K. Quinn to George Meany, May 23, 1957; and Clarence N. Sayen, president, ALPA, to ALPA executive committee, March 27, 1961.

48. George Meany to Clarence N. Sayen, November 17, 1959.

49. "Quill to Contest AFL-CIO Ruling," New York Times, April 9, 1961.

50. Clarence Sayen to ALPA board of directors, August 19, 1960, p. 3; and Quinn interviews. See also Lane Kirkland, executive assistant to the president AFL-CIO, to Kay McMurray, executive vice president, ALPA, March 10, 1961; Clarence Sayen to executive committee, March 27, 1961; Clarence Sayen to George Meany, April 21, 1961; George Meany to Clarence Sayen, July 17, 1961; and Highlights of ALSSA-ALPA-TWU Activities as Taken from Available Records, undated.

51. Air Line Pilots Ass., Internation. v. Air Line Stewards and Stewardesses Association, International, citation memorandum in support of temporary restraining order and preliminary injunction, August 25, 1960; ALSSA, Official Newsletter Affiliated with ALPA, undated (probably August 1960), publication by dissident and severed flight attendants from ALSSA; and Lukas, "Evolution of Flight Attendant Union," p. 20.

52. Quinn interviews; and "Air Steward Union Boss Faces Inquiry," Chicago Sun-Times, July 30, 1963. See also Lukas, "Evolution of Flight Attendant Union," pp. 20–21.

53. Quinn interviews; and Lukas, "Evolution of Flight Attendant Union," p. 21.

54. Report on the Sixteenth Biennial Meeting of the ALPA Board of Directors, independently prepared summary and critical analysis by chairman of Council 51, Eastern Airlines.

55. Interview with Betty Wixted, Chicago, Illinois, March 20, 1981; and Rowland K. Quinn, Jr., to AFL-CIO executive council, undated (probably 1960), p. 5.

56. Berthoud interview.

57. Interview with Charlotte Bunton, Chicago, Illinois, March 20, 1981.

58. George E. Hopkins, The Airline Pilots: A Study in Elite Unionization (Cambridge, Mass.: Harvard University Press, 1971), p. 194.

59. Report by Sally Gibson to interested parties as requested to ALSSA, undated.

60. The Sixteenth Biennial Meeting of the ALPA Board of Directors; and Proceedings of the Sixteenth National Convention of ALPA, November 1960, pp. 842–2286. See also Report of Organizational Structure Study Committee, ALPA Sixteenth Biennial Convention November 14–19, 1960. See also AA MEC newsletter quoted by Paul G. Atkins, AAL MEC; an open letter to the ALPA organizational structure study committee from W. C. Lyndall, ALPA 1st-6958; organizational structure study committee to all members of the ALPA board of directors, July 22, 1960; and Wallace W. Anderson to all members of the board of directors, August 17, 1960.

61. Sixteenth Biennial Meeting of the ALPA Board of Directors, p. 942.

62. Mark Kahn, "Airlines," in *Collective Bargaining: Contemporary American Experience*, edited by Gerald G. Somers (Madison, Wis.: Industrial Relations Research Association, 1980), p. 333, table 6.

63. Proceedings of the Sixteenth National Convention of ALPA, pp. 1666, 1359, 2142–43.

64. Statement of ALSSA in Support of Application for a Charter, p. 25.

65. Opening Remarks to the Sixth Biennial Convention of the Air Line Stewards and Stewardesses Association, International, by Rowland K. Quinn, Jr., president, April 11, 1961, p. 5, in *News Bulletin* 8, 2 (February-March-April 1961).

66. Interview with B. J. Stewart, Los Angeles, California, November 3, 1981.

67. Minutes of AFL-CIO Meeting, June 11, 1961.

68. Lukas, "Evolution of Flight Attendant Union," p. 23.

69. Lane Kirkland to Kay McMurray, March 10, 1961. See also Clarence Sayen, president, ALPA, to ALPA executive committee, March 27, 1961; Clarence Sayen to George Meany, April 21, 1961; George Meany to Clarence Sayen, July 17, 1961; and "Quill to Contest AFL-CIO Ruling," *New York Times*, April 9, 1961.

70. *Air Line Stewards and Stewardesses Assn., Intn'l* v. *N.M.B.*, 294 F.2d 910, 48 LRRM 2623 (D.C. Cir. 1961), *cert. denied*, 369 U.S. 810, 49 LRRM 2743 (1962). See also AFL-CIO jurisdictional claim by ALPA S & S Division, interoffice memo from ALPA M. B. Wiggerson to D. Kidder, September 27, 1963.

71. Quinn interviews.

72. *Flightlog* (published by the S & S Division), May 1972, p. 7. See also National Mediation Board statistics cited in Representation of Flight Attendants on Regional and Trunk Lines and Flight Attendant Labor Organization (p. 3), inhouse documents (Washington, D.C.: Transport Workers Union of America, undated).

73. Quinn interviews.

74. Lukas, "Evolution of Flight Attendant Union," p. 24.

75. "Air Steward Union Boss Faces Inquiry."

76. Lukas, "Evolution of Flight Attendant Union," p. 24.

77. *Air Line Stewards and Stewardesses Association*, Local 550 v. *TWU*, 334 F2d 805 (7th Cir. 1964), *cert. denied* 379 U.S. 972; Quinn interviews; and Lukas, "Evolution of Flight Attendant Union," pp. 25–27.

78. Lukas, "Evolution of Flight Attendant Union," p. 21.

79. Minutes of AFL-CIO Meeting, June 11, 1961.

80. Sixteenth Biennial Meeting of the ALPA Board of Directors; and *Flightlog*, May 1972, p. 7.

Chapter 4

1. Kelly Rueck, "A Time of Change," *Flightlog*, June 1973, pp. 2, 3, 6.

2. Interview with Jack O'Neill, captain, United Airlines, Honolulu, Hawaii, February 28, 1976.

3. Rueck, "A Time of Change."

4. Mary O'Connor, *Flying Mary O'Connor* (New York: Rand McNally and Co., 1961), p. 118.

5. "Stewardess Recruits Much in Demand," *Air Travel*, May 1965, pp. 1–3.

6. Interview with John R. Hill, retired United Airlines legal counsel, Santa Barbara, California, March 7, 1981.

7. Interviews with Edith Lauterbach, San Francisco, California, March 4, 1976, and May 15, 1981.

8. Interview with Sally Watt Keenan, Los Angeles, California, November 2, 1981; and background information written by Keenan on July 11, 1979.

9. Lindsy Van Gelder, "Coffee, Tea, or Me," *Ms.*, January 1973, p. 89.

10. Interviews with Rowland K. Quinn, executive secretary, National Mediation Board, Washington, D.C., February 14, 1979, and March 16, 1981.

11. Decision of United Air Lines System Board of Adjustment, No. 66-1, April 21, 1967.

12. Ibid.

13. Sheldon Rosenberg, "Sex Discrimination and the Labor Arbitration Process," *Labor Law Journal*, February 1979, pp. 103, 116–17.

14. 110 *Congressional Record* 2804–5 (1964), cited in Denis Binder, "Sex Discrimination in the Airline Industry: Title VII Flying High," 59 *California Law Review* 1091 (September 1971): 1092–93.

15. Binder, "Sex Discrimination in the Airline Industry": 1093–96.

16. Kenneth M. Davidson, Ruth B. Ginsburg, Herma H. Kay, *Sex-Based Discrimination: Text: Cases, and Materials* (St. Paul: West Publishing Company, 1974), p. 639. See also *Cooper v. Delta Airlines, Inc.*, 1 Fair Empl. Prac. Cas. 241 (BNA) (Oct. 19, 1967).

17. Binder, "Sex Discrimination in the Airline Industry": 1102, 1103–4.

18. Data supplied by United Airlines industrial relations department, Chicago, Illinois, February 12, 1979.

19. Hill interview.

20. Affidavit of Rachel Woodings in Opposition to Plaintiff's Motion for Partial Summary Judgment, *Elizabeth M. Buckingham et al. v. United Air Lines et al.* (Civil Action No. 71-731-LTL, U.S. District Court, C.D. Cal., 1973).

21. United Airlines Stewardess System Board of Adjustment case no. 66-1; and ibid., quoting Peter Seitz in American Airlines-TWU System Board of Adjustment case, September 15, 1966.

22. Affidavit of Rachel Woodings, *Buckingham v. United Air Lines*.

23. Binder, "Sex Discrimination in the Airline Industry": 1107.

24. *ALPA News, S & S Division* 6, 11 (November 1968): 1.

25. Affidavit of Marty Brown in Opposition to Plaintiff's Motion for Partial Summary Judgment, *Buckingham* v. *United Air Lines.*

26. Ibid., p. 5. See also 1969–71 Agreement between United Air Lines, Inc., and the Air Line Stewardesses and Flight Stewards in the service of United Air Lines, Inc., as represented by the Air Line Pilots Association, International, pp. 92–96.

27. Ten-year statement of consolidated earnings, *UAL, Inc. Annual Report 1973,* p. 25.

28. Data supplied by United Airlines industrial relations department, Chicago, Illinois, February 12, 1979.

29. 1967–1969 Agreement between United Air Lines, Inc. and the Air Line Stewardesses and Flight Stewards in the service of United Air Lines, Inc., as represented by the Air Line Pilots Association, International, p. 8.

30. "ALPA Lawyers Hail Decision against Discrimination by Sex," *S & S News* 8, 8 (September 1970).

31. *Northwest Airlines, Inc.* v. *Transport Workers Union of America, AFL-CIO et al.,* 451 U.S. 77 (1981).

32. *Sprogis* v. *United Airlines,* 308 F. Supp. 959, *aff'd* 444 F.2d 1194, *cert. denied,* 404 U.S. 991.

33. *Romasanta* v. *United Airlines, Inc.,* 537 F.2d 915 (7th Cir. 1975), *aff'd, sub nom. United Airlines* v. *McDonald,* 432 U.S. 385, order dated April 28, 1980; and minutes of the Association of Flight Attendants Local Council 11 meeting for United flight attendants based in San Francisco on January 25, 1980.

34. Interviews with V. Diane Robertson, Foster City, California, January 12, 1979, and August 14, 1980.

35. AFA Council 11 minutes, January 25, 1980.

36. *Romasanta* v. *United Airlines, Inc.,* affidavit of Susan J. Rohde.

37. AFA Council 11 minutes, January 25, 1980.

38. Synopsis of the *McDonald* hearings presented by Nancy Coopersmith to the United Airlines master executive council, Association of Flight Attendants, May 27, 1981.

39. 1969–71 Agreement between United Air Lines, Inc., and the Air Line Stewardesses and Flight Stewards, p. 95.

40. Robertson interviews.

41. Lauterbach interviews; and O'Connor interview.

42. *M. Rosenfeld* v. *United Airlines* (N.Y. Div. H.R. 1975), *aff'd,* 61 A.D.2d 1010 (2d Dept.), 420 N.Y. 2d 630, *appeal denied,* 44 N.Y. 2d 624, *cert. denied,* 99 S. Ct. 571 (1978); and "Pregnant Stewardesses Claim Bias over Rule on Automatic Layoffs," *San Jose Mercury News,* November 25, 1978.

43. "House OK's Pregnant Workers' Bill," *San Francisco Chronicle,* July 19, 1978; "Job Benefits Now Must Cover Pregnancy," *San Francisco Sunday Examiner and Chronicle,* April 4, 1979; Elizabeth Neumeier, counsel, Association of Flight Attendants, to board of directors and executive board, December 1, 1978; and *Flightlog* 16, 4 (December 1978): 18–19.

44. *Burwell* v. *Eastern Airlines, Inc.,* 633 F.2d 361 (4th Cir. 1981).

45. *Harris v. Pan American World Airways, Inc.*, 649 F.2d 670 (9th Cir. 1981).

46. . "Stews Got Pregnant and Lawyers Got Fat," *Honolulu Advertiser*, July 21, 1975, D-5.

47. "The Plight of the Pregnant Flight Attendant," *Flightlog* 12, 9 (October 1974): 3; "Too Fat to Fly?" *Flightlog* 11, 8 (September 1973): 2; and "EEOC Report," *Flightlog* 12, 10 (November-December 1974): 3.

48. Valerie Kincade Oppenheimer, *The Female Labor Force in the United States: Demographic and Economic Factors Governing its Growth and Changing Composition* (Berkeley: University of California Press, 1970), pp. 99, 102, 105, 127; and Cynthia Fuchs Epstein, *Woman's Place* (Berkeley: University of California Press, 1970), pp. 151–66.

49. See *Betty Lou Hunter, Lauretta B. Sanders, Arpe Zadigan et al. v. United Airlines, Inc.*, 10 Fair Empl. Prac. Cas. 787 (Dec. 5, 1979), consent decree.

50. *Diaz v. Pan American World Airways, Inc.*, 311 F. Supp. 559 (S.D. Fla. 1970).

51. Binder, "Sex Discrimination in the Airline Industry": 339.

52. O'Connor, *Flying Mary O'Connor*, pp. 118–19.

53. *Air Line Pilots Association, Int'l v. United Airlines, Inc.*, 480 F. Supp. 1107 (E. D. N.Y. 1979).

54. *Gerdom v. Continental Airlines*, 18 Fair Empl. Prac. Cas. 1118 (C.D. Cal. 1978).

55. Interview with Ragna Roksvag-Zanger, San Francisco, California, May 13, 1981.

56. *Dodd v. American Airlines*, EEOC Dec. (CCH) (1973) ¶6001.

57. Interview with Linda Puchala, president, Association of Flight Attendants, Washington, D.C., March 16, 1981.

58. Robertson interviews.

59. William H. Chafe, *The American Woman: Her Changing Social, Economic, and Political Roles, 1920–1970* (London: Oxford University Press, 1972), pp. 226–54.

Chapter 5

1. AFA Study Committee Report, compiled to comply with a resolution made at a special board of directors meeting, June 6–7, 1974.

2. *S & S News* 8, 11 (December 1970); and *Western News* (published by Western Airlines Master Executive Council), Winter 1971.

3. Transcript of Proceedings, Air Line Pilots Association, Stewards and Stewardesses Division, Board of Directors Meeting, Las Vegas, Nevada, December 3, 1972, p. 1104.

4. Telephone interview with George E. Hopkins, May 31, 1981.

5. Interview with Jack Bavis, executive secretary of Air Line Pilots Association, Washington, D.C., March 18, 1981; and telephone interview with Jack Bavis, May 13, 1981.

6. "J. J. O'Donnell Succeeds Charles Ruby to ALPA Presidency," *Western News*, Winter 1971, p. 2.

7. Bavis interviews; and *Western News*, Winter 1971, p. 3.

8. "1969–1974: The Evolution of Strength," presented by Association of Flight Attendants president Kelly Rueck at the June 4, 1974, meeting of the excecutive board, reprinted in *Flightlog* 12, 7 (August-September 1974): 3.

9. Transcript of Proceedings, Air Line Pilots Association, Stewards and Stewardesses Division, Special Board of Directors Meeting, Washington, D.C., October 10, 1973, p. 63.

10. Interview with Barbara Rideout, member of *Flightlog* staff, Association of Flight Attendants, Washington, D.C., February 23, 1976.

11. Interview with Shirley Shimon, United Airlines flight attendant, Georgetown, Colorado, January 28, 1977; interviews with V. Diane Robertson, Foster City, California, January 12, 1979, and August 14, 1980; and interview with Fran Hay, former secretary-treasurer, Association of Flight Attendants, Washington, D.C., January 27, 1979.

12. Bavis interviews.

13. Interviews with Delfina Mott, Washington, D.C., January 23, 1979, and November 20, 1979; and Transcript of Proceedings, Air Line Pilots Association, Special Meeting of the Board of Directors, Stewards and Stewardesses Division, Denver, Colorado, June 27, 1973, pp. 181–86.

14. Kelly Rueck, vice president, S & S Division, ALPA, to Beate Bloch, associate solicitor, U.S. Department of Labor, February 8, 1973; Beate Bloch to Kelly Rueck, March 23, 1973; and Michael H. Gottesman to Kelly Rueck, March 13, 1973. See also Michael H. Gottesman to Beate Bloch, Esq., associate solicitor, June 18, 1973; and Michael H. Gottesman to Kelly Rueck, March 12, 1973.

15. Beate Bloch to Kelly Rueck, March 23, 1973.

16. ALPA chronology, pp. 8–10; "Stewardesses to Remain Part of ALPA 'for Time Being,'" *Aviation Daily*, October 15, 1973, p. 2; "ALPA Pilots, Stewardesses at Impasse," *Aviation Daily*, October 16, 1973; and "Stewardesses Want Own Union," *Aviation Daily*, November 6, 1973.

17. TWA master executive council, ALPA, to J. J. O'Donnell, August 17, 1973.

18. Eastern master executive council, ALPA, to J. J. O'Donnell, September 6, 1973.

19. George E. Berg to J. J. O'Donnell, August 10, 1973.

20. Telephone interview with Kelly Rueck Pike, former president of the Association of Flight Attendants, Leesburg, Virginia, January 23, 1979. See also AFA Study Committee Report, p. 4.

21. Transcript of Proceedings, Air Line Pilots Association, Stewards and Stewardesses Division, Sixth Executive Board Meeting, Washington, D.C., May 16, 1973, pp. 282–83.

22. Bavis interviews.

23. Transcript of Proceedings, Air Line Pilots Association, Stewards and Stewardesses Division, Special Meeting of the Board of Directors, Denver, Colorado, June 26, 1973, pp. 19–22.

24. Ibid., pp. 26–50, 86–100; and Report of the Stewards and Stewardesses Division Study Committee, cover letter by Kelly Rueck (May 1973), pp. 35–47, 99.

25. Ibid., pp. 103–4; George Meany, president, AFL-CIO, to Clarence Sayen, president, ALPA, May 16, 1961; George Meany to AFL-CIO national and international union presidents, January 19, 1963, regarding article 21 of the AFL-CIO constitution and bylaws; and M. B. Wiggerson to D. B. Kidder, vice president, ALPA (S & S Division), memorandum on AFL-CIO jurisdictional claim by ALPA S & S Division vs. TWU, September 27, 1963.

26. J. J. O'Donnell, president, ALPA, and Kelly Rueck, vice president, Stewards and Stewardesses Division, Memorandum of Understanding, November 1, 1973; and Kelly Rueck, vice president, and Maggie Jacobsen, secretary, S & S Division, to the S & S board of directors, November 3, 1973. See also Kelly Rueck to all steward and stewardess membership, November 9, 1973; Resolution, Agreement Establishing Autonomy and Affiliation of Stewards and Stewardesses Division, Administrative Agreement, and Constitution and By-Laws (undated), pp. 1–16.

27. Agreement Establishing Autonomy and Affiliation of Stewards and Stewardesses Division, December 31, 1973.

28. ALPA chronology, pp. 11–12.

29. Rowland K. Quinn, executive secretary, to Edward J. Hickey, Jr., December 4, 1974; and Edward J. Hickey, Jr., counsel for AFA study committee, to George S. Ives, chairman, National Mediation Board, September 3, 1974.

30. *Flightlog* 13, 3 (August 1975): 7.

31. *Flightlog* 17, 1 (Spring 1979): 12a.

32. Kelly Rueck to the board of directors and executive board, reprinted in *Flightlog* 14, 1 (January-February 1976): 4.

33. "1969–1974: The Evolution of Strength."

34. Hay interview.

35. Kelly Rueck, "President's Message," *Flightlog* 13, 3 (June-July 1975): 2.

Chapter 6

1. See "Hot Pants, Cleavage, Booze, Sexy Airline Flying High," *San Francisco Chronicle*, April 5, 1978.

2. *Daily Labor Report*, June 25, 1974.

3. *Daily Labor Report*, June 24, 1974.

4. "Safety Board Would Act before Accidents Happen," *Aviation Daily*, March 22, 1977.

5. Telephone interview with Nancy Williams, Sausalito, California, April 6, 1979.

6. Ibid.

7. Telephone interviews with Susan Rohde, master executive council chairperson for United Airlines, Association of Flight Attendants, San Francisco, California, April 14, 1979, and March 10, 1981.

8. Williams interview.

9. Rohde interviews.

10. Interviews with Charles W. Thomson, director, industrial relations, United Airlines, Inc., Elk Grove Township, Illinois, February 12, 1979, and March 19, 1981.

11. Williams interview.

12. Rohde interviews.

13. Thomson interviews.

14. Edward E. Carlson, chairman of the board, United Airlines, Inc., to flight attendants, February 4, 1975.

15. Thomson interviews.

16. *Air Line Pilots Association, International* v. *United Airlines, Inc.*, 8 Fair Empl. Prac. Cas. 1117, affidavits of Mary Lyn Moseley and Joan Simms, March 17, 1975.

17. Order to show cause and temporary restraining order, 75C 399, United States District Judge Bramwell, Brooklyn, New York, March 17, 1975.

18. Rohde interviews.

19. Interviews with V. Diane Robertson, Foster City, California, January 12, 1979, and August 14, 1980.

20. Rohde interviews.

21. Interview with Susan Bianchi Sand, Washington, D.C., March 17, 1981.

22. Interview with Duane M. Buckmaster, Elk Grove, Illinois, March 19, 1981.

23. Mark L. Kahn, "Labor-Management Relations in the Airline Industry," in *The Railway Labor Act at Fifty* (Washington, D.C.: U.S. Government Printing Office, 1977), pp. 119–20.

24. "85.9% for Contract Ratified," *Agenda* 6, 1 (March 1976).

25. Agreement between United Airlines, Inc., and Air Line Stewardesses, as Represented by the Air Line Stewardesses Association, January 1, 1946; and Agreement between United Airlines, Inc., and Association of Flight Attendants, 1974–77.

26. Robertson interviews.

27. UAL and AFA Agreement, 1974–77, section 4A, p. 13.

28. Transcript of Proceedings, Air Line Pilots Association, Stewards and Stewardesses Division, Sixth Executive Board Meeting, Washington, D.C., May 16, 1973, p. 282.

29. "Looking Back," *Free Press* (Union of Flight Attendants), March 1981, pp. 24–25.

30. Bianchi Sand interview.

31. Kathy Hutchens to AFA Local Council 11 meeting, September 1977.

32. Thomson interviews.

33. Data supplied by Jean Widenmyer, director of accounting and membership, Association of Flight Attendants.

34. Interview with Alice Flynn, president, Independent Union of Flight Attendants (IUFA), Burlingame, California, April 24, 1981.

35. Interview with Judy Malone, Washington, D.C., May 13, 1981.

36. Summary of 1980–82 Tentative Agreement, undated (distributed April 1980).

37. Interviews with Irene Eastin, San Francisco, California, March 6 and 11, 1981.

38. Data supplied by Jean Widenmyer, AFA.

39. Data supplied by Jean Widenmyer, AFA, from April 1, 1981, inventory, and by Francine Zucker, director, communications, AFA, April 19, 1982.

40. Data supplied by Helen Schalet, research analyst, Association of Flight Attendants, April 7, 1981. See also AFA *Summary of Flight Attendant Agreements* (Washington, D.C.: Association of Flight Attendants, 1981, table 1, p. 1.

41. Flynn interview.

42. Data supplied by Helen Schalet. See also *Free Press*, March 1981, p. 23.

43. "Flight Attendants Break Away from Union," *New York Times*, August 1, 1978. See also "TWA Flight Attendants to Vote on New Union," *Aviation Daily*, January 4, 1977; and Kathy Lukas, "The Evolution of the Flight Attendant Movement in the United States" (paper for Department of Social Sciences, San Francisco State University), pp. 32–42.

44. Flynn interview.

45. "President's Message: The Myth of the Independent Union," *Flightlog* 15, 2 (March 1977).

46. *New York Times*, August 1, 1978.

47. Interview with Pamela Casey, Washington, D.C., March 17, 1981; and Secretary-Treasurer Pamela Casey to the fifth board of directors, Association of Flight Attendants, Los Angeles, California, November 3, 1980, p. 5.

48. Interview with Linda Puchala, president, AFA, Washington, D.C., March 16, 1981; Bianchi Sand interview; Casey interview; and interviews with Kathy Hutchens, San Francisco, California, April 3, 1979, September 5, 1980, and March 2 and 24, 1981.

49. Hutchens interviews.

50. Address to the Board of Directors, Association of Flight Attendants, undated and unsigned (entered into the transcript of proceedings official record November 3, 1979).

51. Hutchens interviews.

52. Ibid.

Index

Army Air Corps, 13
Arnott, Margaret, 10
Association of Flight Attendants (AFA),
xix, xxi, xxii, 3, 125, 131; and early
effects of deregulation, 135–36; factions
within, 126; founded, 114–15, 118; internal politics, 134–35; and litigation of
women's issues, 91–95, 99–100, 101;
presidential recall, 134–35; representation, 131–32; structure, 134; vulnerability, 127
Association of Professional Flight Attendants (APFA), 3; representation,
132–33. *See also* American Airlines

Baker, Terry Van Horn, 88
Berg, George, 111
Behncke, David L., 24, 33–34, 35, 55,
70; influence on legislation, 26–30
Berne, Eric, 97
Berthoud, Paul, 62; on agency shop, 65
Bianchi, Susan, 118, 123, 128–29, 135
Black, Hugo, 13
Blue Book, 1977–80 agreement between
AFA and UAL, 128, 129, 130
Boeing Air Transport, 3, 7, 8; sky girl ex-
periment, 7–10
Boeing trimotor, 7, 10
Bona fide occupational qualification
(BFOQ), 85, 98, 117
Braniff Airlines, 33, 77, 132; bankruptcy,
132; no-marriage rule, 88
Brotherhood of Rail, Airline, and Steam-
ship Clerks, Freight Handlers, Express
and Station Employees (BRAC), 112
Brown, Ada J., 3, 31–54, 46–49, 62, 79,
124, 125; conflict with ALPA leaders,
33–35, 45
Brown, William Folger, 5–6, 13
Buckmaster, Duane, 122, 125

Capital Airlines, 55, 66, 81. *See also* Cen-
tral Airlines and Pennsylvania Central
Airlines
Carter, Jessie, 10, 11
Caribbean Airlines, 10

Casey, Pamela, 135
Central Airlines, 9. *See also* Capital Air-
lines and Pennsylvania Central Airlines
Chase, Helen, 69, 78
Church, Ellen, 7–8, 9–12, 23
Citizens Advisory Council on the Status of
Women, 85
Civil Aeronautics Act of 1938, 14
Civil Aeronautics Administration: first
safety regulations for flight attendants,
17–18; and flights without flight atten-
dants, 25
Civil Aeronautics Board, 15
Civil Aeronautics Regulation (CAR),
17–18
Civil Rights Act of 1964, Title VII, *xvii,
xxii,* 3, 19, 81, 85, 86–87, 117
Coalition of Labor Union Women
(CLUW), *xxi*
Colvin v. Piedmont Airlines, 86
Commercial aviation, early history, 4–6,
7, 9
Congress of Industrial Organizations
(CIO). *See* American Federation of La-
bor–Congress of Industrial Organiza-
tions
Continental Airlines, 3, 33, 100–11, 117,
126
Cooper, Eulalie E., 85
Cooper v. Delta Airlines, 85–86
Craft, Frances Hall. *See* Hall, Frances
Crawford, Ellis, 10
Curtis, Jesse W., 100

Davis, Roland C., 44
DC-3, 15–16, 24
DeCelles, Joseph, 73
Delta Airlines, 2, 85
Diaz v. Pan American World Airways,
96–98
Dodd v. American Airlines, 101

Eastern Airlines, 10–11, 13, 25; flight attendants in ALSSA, 59, 63; no-marriage rule, 19, 84; no-pregnancy rule,
95; pilots, 111

Eastin, Irene, 48, 55, 56
Equal Pay Amendment to the Fair Labor
  Standards Act, 59
Equal Employment Opportunity Com-
  mission, 85–88, 89, 96
Ethnic hiring policies, 30, 45, 81
Exploitation of flight attendants in adver-
  tising, *xxi*, 1, 81–82, 101, 117

Farley, James, 13
Federal Aviation Authority, 61
Federal Aviation Regulation (FAR),
  17–18, 25, 61, 131
Federal Aviation Administration (FAA),
  131
First flight attendants, 10
Fitzsimmons, Frank, 66
Flight Engineers International Associa-
  tion, 64
Flight Pursers and Stewardesses, 47
Flying Tiger, 132
Friedan, Betty, 52
Frontier Airlines, 9, 76, 132
Fruite, Inez Keller. *See* Keller, Inez
Fry, Harriet, 10

Gibson, Sally, 71
Gledhill, Franklin, 46
Green, William, 53
Green Book, 1974–77 contractual agree-
  ment between AFA and UAL, *xix*
  124–25, 128
Greenfield, Ada J. Brown. *See* Brown,
  Ada J.

Hall, Frances, 31, 33, 36, 38–39, 41, 48
Hall, Sally Thometz. *See* Thometz, Sally
Hardy, Darenda, 126–27
Hawaiian Airlines, 132; no-marriage rule,
  76, 84
Hay, Fran, 116
Health, and jet travel, 65
Heisler, Janet, 69, 78
Herbert, Victor, J., 18, 48, 55, 57–59, 60
Hill, John R., 21, 32, 36–39, 44–45
Hofe, Albert, 11

Hoffa, Jimmy, 66
Holmes, Fran, 71
Hughes, Howard, 62
Hutchens, Kathy, 129, 136

Independent Federation of Flight Atten-
  dants (IFFA), 3, 132–33
Independent Union of Flight Attendants
  (IUFA), 3, 130, 132–33
International Association of Machinists
  and Aerospace Workers (IAMAW), 46,
  112, 123
International Brotherhood of Teamsters
  (IBT), 66–67, 112–13, 126, 127
International Guild of Flight Attendants,
  70

Johnson, Alva, 10
Johnson, E. H., 36–37, 42
Johnson, Phil, 9

Kahn, Mark L., 124
Katzell, Raymond, 97
Keller, Inez, 10–11
Kelly, Clyde, 4
Kelly Act, 4
Koos, Mary Alice, 55–60

Labor-Management Reporting and Dis-
  closure Act (LMRDA), 53, 54; chal-
  lenge to its constitutionality, 54, 68,
  70, 73, 75, 78–79, 110
Laffey, Mary, 91
Landrum, Philip, 53–54
Landrum-Griffin Act. *See* Labor-Manage-
  ment Reporting and Disclosure Act
Lake Central Airlines, 63
Lauterbach, Edith, 16, 30, 33, 37, 38, 42,
  62, 66; and first grievance to system
  board, 44–45
Law, Ruth, 8
Leibik and Weyland, 78
Lindberg, Charles, 5
Littler and Coakley, 36

McCall, Marge, 22
McCarthyism, 53